If I'm Prince

MW01534165

Kissing Frogs?

By

Ilinda M.J. Reese

Netwic publishing - Willoughby, Ohio

Third Edition

If I'm Looking For A Prince, Why Am I Kissing Frogs?

© 1998 by Ilinda M.J. Reese

Published by Netwic

Distributed by IMJ ReeSources

3725 Lee Road

Shaker Heights, Ohio 44120

(216) 561-4657 fax (216) 991-7209

ISBN: 0-942923-08-1

Front cover and illustrations created by Clifferd E. Lee

Detroit, Michigan

Edited by Lea Leever Oldham

Printed in the United States of America

CONTENTS

PART III. HOW TO KEEP IT IF YOU GOT IT

Transition Specialist & Author

- Dynamic
- Informative
- Humorous
- Intellectual
- Genuine

IMJ REESOURCES

Introducing "The Transition Physician"
ILINDA J. REESE

Ilinda Reese is author of the book "If I'm Looking For A Prince, Why Am Still Kissing Frogs " and lecturer for the Better Way Institute. Ms. Reese is also in the process of expanding her own company called IMJ Reesources. She is a veteran of company transition and personal development. Ilinda speaks impressively drawing from over fifteen years of corporate field experience. Ilinda is now available for seminars, workshop and speaking engagements. Candid, sophisticated and humorous, characterizes a productive, enlightening and exciting day with Cleveland's own "Transition Physician" Ilinda Reese.

ACHIEVEMENTS-
- INTERNATIONAL SPEECH COMPETITION / WINNER
- SILVER BOWL (GLASGOW, SCOTLAND) / WINNER
- REGIONAL ITC SPEECH COMPETITION / 3 TIME WINNER
- W.A.V.E. HUMANITARIAN AWARD / WINNER

AFFILIATIONS-
- ITC (INTERNATIONAL TRAINING IN COMMUNICATION) / MEMBER
- NATIONAL SPEAKERS ASSOCIATION / MEMBER
- WORTH SHARING COMMUNICATIONS / MEMBER
- COVENANT COMMUNITY OF CLEVELAND / MEMBER

*For reservations, seminars, workshops, & keynotes. Prescriptions for Transition Call (216) 561-4657
Another service of The Better Way Institute (216) 991-1155

EGP Media, Inc. The Official Ad Agency of The Better Way Institute

FOREWORD

The challenge of boy/girl relationship is just as perplexing today as it has ever been. Each is on an individual journey through life with all the stuff that goes with it. However, each brings qualities, abilities, physical, mental and emotional attractions to the relationship.

The best I've been able to understand, with the help of Ilinda's great book, is one must choose his/her level of happiness, direction and purpose of life. To the extent of responsibility for that happiness is shouldered, each partner has a great chance for a strong enduring, fulfilling relationship.

To the extent you know yourself, know what you want and how to understand to a reasonable degree, how the opposite sex works--a great relationship is definitely possible.

Great job Ilinda!

Lucius L. Lewis
Is President and Founder of the Better Way Institute and author of a Better Way of Taking Care of You.

Dedication

I express my heartfelt thanks and gratitude to the following:

TO GOD:

All thanks to God from whom all blessings flow, who lovingly gives every good and perfect gift. It is He that gives me the passionate desire, ability and perseverance to complete this project. I acknowledge my Lord and Savior Jesus Christ to whom all honor is due.

TO MY SPECIAL FRIENDS,

Not to immortalize their names or increase book sales but because they really are "special" people. They have been the wind beneath my wings that continually lifts me to new heights.

To a powerful group of speakers who recognized my limitless potential and who helped the vision become a reality. Thank you members of Worth Sharing Communications: **Theresa Anderson** (author/entrepreneur), **Horace David Bey, Sandra Bishop, Darnell Carter, William Dawson, Brenda Ellis, Cassie Lewis,** and **Nina Turner,** in particular, **SeMia Bray** (author/entrepreneur) without her assistance the project would have been an overwhelming task, **Henry Ford** (author), and **Lucius Lewis** (author/entrepreneur and the wind beneath my wings), who knew how hard to push. Without you this venture would not be a reality. Each meeting with you caused me to believe I could leap tall buildings in a single bound. To the extension of the group, author and speaker, **Patricia Weingard-Carson,** "the Dream Team," Dr. **Robert Lawson,** (Ph.D./author) and **Aleta Mays,** (author), thank you for your continued guidance and strong support. To my Mentor, **George Fraser** (author/entrepreneur), thank you for your willingness to share your wisdom and experience with me.

To **Debra Landrum,** my best friend, not only in word but also in deed. She is a person that does not only talk the talk but walks the walk. She is the spirit behind many projects, the results of which you see. Thank you for being you, sister friend.

8

To **Albert R. Donald**, who came along at a time when I was most vulnerable, helped to stabilize my thoughts and to realize there is a beautiful black woman inside me. Thank you for always being there and becoming my best friend.

To my associate and friend, **Phillip Cole**, who deserves applause for his insights and explanations of my behavior (no small matter). Your enlightenment gave me courage to look at the truth regardless of the outcome. For your commitment, diligence, attention to proofing, and critiquing the written text, Thank you Phil.

I would especially like to **thank my family**. My dad, **Lawrence W. Boone**, Pastor of Covenant Community of Cleveland and my mom, **Theresa B. Boone,** First Lady (she says "the only lady") for providing and reinforcing principles for living. Most importantly, thank you for teaching and developing my love for Jesus Christ. To my children: **Tammy Williams**, **Eric,** and **Raffael Reese**, **Mark Williams** (son-in-law), sister and brothers, **Cynthia, Clayton** and **Ronald Boone**, thank you. Thank you for loving me unconditionally and providing support through the difficult times of my life.

Thank you **Covenant Community** family for standing by my side and supporting my efforts with words of encouragement. To the young women of Covenant Community, this is for you. Listen, learn and grow. I love you.

To my **Aunt Marion Bryant** and **Cousin Emma Lowry,** two people who recognized value and returned my misplaced manuscript, my undying gratitude. Thank you both.

Thank you to Deborah Kerr, Carol Meyer and **Barb Pace** (thank you for the late nights and diligence to a difficult task) for their assistance, clerical support, and for just being friends.

There are numerous friends and family that have not been mentioned. It is not because anyone is more important than another is. This is to say "Thank you" to everyone that has contributed in anyway to the quality of my life.

To my daughter and friend, **Quiana Marché' Pettigrew**, to who I hope to pour my life into, thank you for "keeping it real."

Ilinda M.J. Reese
3725 Lee Road
Shaker Heights, Ohio 44120

INTRODUCTION

This book is to serve as a *wake-up* call to **women of all ages**. Its purpose is to awaken and empower women (by raising their consciousness) to their responsibility to make correct choices in relationships. **If I'm Looking For A Prince, Why Am I Still Kissing Frogs***?* supplies the how-tos of successful selection and maintenance of meaningful relationships.

This book will not tell you anything you have not heard before, in one form or another. There are several excellent books on the market and speakers on the circuit (a few are in the reading list) that have similar messages and information. If I had read several of the best-selling books in their entirety, I would feel there is no need to write another book on "relationships." During the creation of this project, frequently while watching television, I heard information that caused me to respond. My comments included: "Hey, that's from my book or I said that." Since it is true that a wealth of information exists, why, I ask, do the problems continue to exist? Why are relationships a constant source of trouble, more than the center of pleasure?

The search for the answers led to the research and writing of **If I'm Looking For A Prince, Why Am I Still Kissing Frogs?** Through this work, I can testify to what years of research and studies have taught me and present the information in a style that is uniquely my own. Shakespeare once said, "Life is a twice-told story."

A childhood friend of mine at one point had married four or five times. I lost count. Her response to my question, as to why she kept becoming married, was "I will keep trying until I get it right."

The contents of the book, **If I'm Looking For A Prince, Why Am I Still Kissing Frogs,** was compiled from various sources. As a trainer and workshop facilitator by trade, opportunities to work with diverse population occurred weekly.

The information contained represents:

Countless informally held conversations between women and men, Counseling sessions (professional and personal) and experiences shared by women and men wrapped in despair.

Feeling a sense of urgency, this book is in response to the frequent wail of women who ask, "Where have all the good men gone?" Why haven't I gotten one? Or met *him*? "Will I ever meet *him*?"

These conversations usually end with a smile on their face but looking deeper, one can see the pain in their eyes. Though the majority of the information contained is applicable to both genders, this book is for women, to women, about women, from a woman. A kind of woman-to-woman conversation. In most cases, the book's text is written utilizing generalities. The terminology used -- women, men -- are indicative of the observable actions and/or beliefs of a large percentage. It is not to infer the inclusively of *all*. If you believe you are the exception (based on the topic being discussed), you have only to look over your shoulder to find someone to whom it applies.

The ▲ symbol displayed through out the book represents a time to reflect. The symbol represents a time to think and to challenge your preconceived ideas. Pause to record your thoughts and insights. Take the time to review what you have written. Do not attempt to expedite time or cheat by skipping the questions. The pyramid represents disconnected thought, questions that interrupt your normal thought patterns.

Accept the task to work through the practical steps. Each chapter is self-contained and can be utilized individually or for group discussion.

If I'm Looking For A Prince, Why Am I Still Kissing Frogs? is for the "emotionally challenged" and could be called a book of questions. Someone once said, "When we are sufficiently tired of getting wrong answers from society, we will seek the right answers from our own essence."

It asks no hard questions, only honest ones. Do not be afraid of the questions. The questions are presented to raise your consciousness. They are practical steps to assist you in the evaluation and measurement of your personal development. Not everyone will agree, accept the principles, or be willing to do the work necessary. To those who accept the challenge, it is the author's hope it will aid in your growth.

If I'm Looking For A Prince, Why Am I Still Kissing Frogs is divided into (3) parts.

Part I establishes a foundation for the realities of the present state of relationships. It provides an explanation of the socialization process and the results.

Part II looks at the search for love and how to get it if you want it. The chapters under this heading cover the Dating game, the Art of self-acceptance, and How to create a more marketable you.

Part III focuses on the basic How-tos of maintaining a relationship. This section provides a description of what a healthy relationship looks like. Most often couples find themselves trying to live up to an idealized version created by the media versus understanding what it means to be in a relationship.

The objective is not to provide a forum for "bashing or blaming" men for the sad state of affairs. There is no shortage of places where the blame could be assigned. This is not the focal point. The focus is to provide an opportunity to take a fresh look at an old problem in a new way. It is to:

♦ Facilitate discussion.
♦ Create honest dialogue.
♦ Make possible a healing between the sexes.

The examples attempt to explain the relationship puzzle. Yet even normal, daily interactions create misunderstandings. It's okay if you feel the urge to say, "I know you're right." Committed relationships are as difficult as that of two porcupines. As the two porcupines attempt to come together out of a need to get warm, they feel the painful pricks of their quills. The closer they get to each other, the more painful the experience

13

becomes. **If I'm Looking For A Prince, Why Am I Still Kissing Frogs?** acknowledges that getting relationships right takes a lifetime of enormous challenges. Yet the journey can be a boundless continuum of joy.

The book is written not only for singles in search of love, but also for those presently in relationships. Before men and women can be successful at achieving relationships, it is necessary to understand how they work, and how what we do and believe can enhance or destroy them.

Understanding the process can assist one to:
♦ Break the tendency to continually re-play the same tape.
♦ Escape the repeating of the same emotional mistakes.
♦ Prevent emotionally draining and empty associations.

The situations may be painfully recognizable and bring to mind persons known or unknown. The names have been changed to protect the desperate and any similarities between persons known and unknown are purely coincidental and unintended. The problems and challenges dealt with are relevant for all races and genders.

Every attempt has been made to identify the original source of quotations and illustrations used, to give proper credit to the author. Any additional information supplied regarding the source or origin of a piece will be included in the second printing of the book.

As the author, I have attempted to step outside myself, so as not to dilute the information with my own fears, prejudices, and experiences. Of course, this was an impossible task. As a motivational speaker by trade, I believe in the importance of sharing one's self. One writer pointed out we become bolder when we share our fears, richer by sharing our losses, wiser by admitting our errors and closer by sharing ourselves.

It is my hope that, the style of the presentation will give insight into the experiences that shaped the thoughts, ideas, and the personal effect the information has had on me. The book could have been called, "Lessons I Learned the Hard Way, But You Don't Have

To." If the truth were known, I am still learning the lessons. Life is a great teacher.

In the End:

We will conserve only what we love,

We will love only what we understand,

We will understand only what

We are taught.

(Anonymous)

It is my desire that you will grow from the words you read, and be a better person because of the encounter.

CHAPTER 1

THE FAIRY TALE

(The Approach)

Once upon a time there was a princess. She, a lady In waiting, had spent her entire lifetime preparing to meet her prince. Her style spoke elegance and revealed that much effort was put into her appearance. Her hair was perfectly coifed and makeup just right. The princess' persona exuded confidence and self-assurance. When she spoke, her soft, sexy voice emanated a quiet dignity. She dressed up any scene and any man would be proud to have her on his arm. On this particular day, the princess, while walking unattended in the garden, stumbled over something sitting in her path.

(Conversation)

Startled she looked down and simultaneously heard a voice say, "What's a beautiful girl like you doing walking alone in the garden?" After a few moments of desperate searching for the source of the voice, the princess eyes returned to and settled on the only object on the path.

A FROG

A green, tailless, web-footed frog, warts and all. After the initial shock diminished, curiosity got the best of her. Flattered by his words and apparent intellectual perception of her inner beauty, she continued the conversation. She began asking intimate questions about his state of affairs. "What gave you the ability to speak?" the princess asked. The question, the first of many, led her deeper into the emotional abyss. The frog spoke of his previous status, that of a handsome prince, adored by the people of his kingdom, with one exception. There had been one filled with grievous envy and resentment of his acts of kindness. An evil one who used her powers, (to fulfill her need for revenge) to curse him to an existence lower than that of his royal birthright. Hearing the frog's story, the princess quickly developed an emotional attachment.

(Manipulative Flattery)

Subconsciously his words fed into her innate need to nurture and protect.

"I need you" the frog continued, "You can help me. I've never seen one so beautiful as you and I'm completely under your spell. The magic of this moment is so intoxicating. I know if you'll *kiss* me, I'll change into a *prince*. At least that is what the fairy tales say."

By this time his eloquent words and charm, combined with her need to nurture, had her hooked.

The princess quickly discarded the thought that she had not had time to get to know the frog or explore why she was even talking to a frog. *How could she* determine the level of truth being spoken?

(Expectations)

The princess, unaware that the frog's flowery words were only generalities, continued to be intrigued by him. The frog's only intent was to get her to kiss him. His focus, the completion of his goal, was to get what he wanted most: Physical release.

Wanting to believe that she had finally met her prince, she acted. Without hesitation she picked up the frog and laid one on him. *Nothing* happened! Again she tried, this time giving more of herself with no results.

(The Guilt Trip)

She began thinking, I must be doing something wrong. It must be my technique. Maybe if I **change** my style or approach, he'll change.

18

(The Blame Game)

Try as she might, at the end of the day, the gardener found her weeping bitterly, for having been abandoned by the frog. The princess could still hear his accusations ringing in her ears as he hopped away. His poignant, cutting words said, "If you were a real Princess, it would have worked. I guess you don't have what it takes to meet my needs." Now she sat, full of resentment, harboring feelings of inadequacy and guilt. What did she expect from a frog? After all, he was still a frog. *(A Frog is a Frog, is a Frog.)*

Are you wondering why a book on relationships would begin with a fairy tale? Let me clarify. Though this story may remind you of a familiar fairy tale you read as a child, this same scenario is played out every day. It occurs over and over and over in the lives of ordinary women. Women who spend their lives looking for a man, not just any man, but a good man. Although the techniques being used, in this instance, are clearly labeled, the manipulative tools are usually so subtle they go unnoticed.

Unlike the original version of the fairy tale published in 1812, the frog in this newly created version is acutely aware that he is a frog. He never was, nor will be, a prince. *Favorite Fairy Tales, describes fairy tales are stories that talk about basic human emotions. This involves all of us.

In the original version, the expectation of the frog was that the princess had the power to transform him with a kiss. With a kiss of compassion, the spell would be broken and he would return to his former self. After all, he was a prince that had been cursed to exist in this horrible, lonely state by a wicked fairy. Not so in this modern-day analogy. In this book, the fantasy does not change the reality that a frog is a frog.

*Favorite Fairy Tales compiled by Cooper Edens and Harold Darling of Blue Lantern Studio

CHAPTER 2

A LADY IN WAITING

Social Conditioning

"Then the princess opened her eyes and held out her hand to the prince, saying, joyfully,

"Oh, I've been waiting such a long time for you to come and wake me."

It does not matter how long the waiting has been. Whether 20, 30, or 40 years, the lady waits for it and longs for it. She desires to be held, protected, and touched by that special someone. Ask any young girl to tell you about her wedding plans and, in all probability, you will receive detailed specifics of her vision. She can probably tell you the color scheme, what she will wear, and where the wedding and honeymoon will take place. Try it! Females grow up thinking about it even before establishing a committed relationship. They begin looking to Prince Charming or Mr. Right for happiness.

Not only are the young guilty of hopeful pre-planning. One conscientious female, early 40's reports having identified the caterer and coordinator she will use, yet admittedly, there are no serious prospects in her present picture. Check your college campuses if you need additional documentation of serious search techniques. What is the origin of this thought pattern? Let's review the socialization process of the average female to see if there are any clues. So where does the idea come from?

The female has been told all of her life, through one form or another, that romantic love has the magical power to make one happy and whole. The typical female child grows up on a steady diet of fairy tales. Fairy tales whose common theme appears to be "and they lived happily ever after." The thread that continually weaves throughout the stories says, "Look to a man for the solution to your problems."

A quick trip to the library and a review of fairy tales will awaken you to the consistent theme. Fairy tales like, Cinderella, Sleeping Beauty, Snow White (who sang "Someday my Prince will come" in the Disney movie version), and Rapunzel. Recently a cartoonist portrayed a more accurate picture when his illustration displayed a mother sitting beside her daughter's bed reading the Cinderella fairy tale. The daughter looked up at the mother and said, "Tell me the part where Cinderella and Prince Charming have been married for a while and start to get on each other's nerves!" Someone once said, "It begins when you sink into his arms and ends with your arms in the sink."

Through social conditioning, females learn about their role. According to researchers, these early patterns, though undergoing modification, carry into adulthood. Citing the role parents play in raising their children along gender lines, Drs'. Rhodes and Goldner support the theory that even before a baby is born, the parents are pre-programming its sex. The sex-specific socialization results in the sexes being raised differently. Today's Black Woman, April 1997).

Not only is the conditioning from those within her environment (parents, relatives, teachers), but the influences from games, books, films, and other media forms are strongly felt. Bombardment of messages through songs, such as, "You're nobody till somebody loves you" and "Stand by your man," reinforce the message, "you *need a man*." Literature, television, media, and movies help reinforce this belief.

The movie "Mahogany" created the words spoken by Billie Dee, "Success is nothing without someone to share it with."

Most girls are brought up on nursery rhymes. You remember... Joe and Janey sitting in a tree, K*I*S*S*I*N*G, first comes love, then comes marriage, then comes Janey with a baby carriage. The names are not important. They were interchangeable but the message stood alone.

If that is not enough, the female child receives the same message from her household. The conditioning process from a mother or sister included statements that said, "Women need to downplay their intellect, let the boys/men win the games, don't let them see how smart you are." Oh yes, things are changing but not quickly enough to turn around the present.

In the April 1991 issue of <u>Working Woman</u> magazine, a game called "Careers for Girls" was described as "the fame, fortune, and happiness game." This description is not from the author of the article but the producers of the game, Parker Bros. The writer of the article, Gail Collins, a columnist and author, describes the game as, "The second most depressing board game I have ever seen."

The article mentioned the writer's first choice, "The Trump." The misleading name, "Career for Girls," entices a person to believe the game promotes career exploration. The target population indicated the game is designed for girl's 8-12 years old. Careers included as options are: Fashion Designer, Rock Star, College Graduate, Schoolteacher, and "Super" Mom. Wait, before you begin following the thinking pattern that says, "the careers listed are honorable ones," let's look at the descriptions provided by the game and the messages being implied through the suggested careers.

Super Mom -

Not because she has a career and manages to keep a balance between home and family, as a great number of women presently are doing. No, "super" because she has eight children. A child selecting this career path would receive instructions that require her to: Begin to select and focus on her dream husband. Another card speaks to her cooking skills (she loses a turn for having burned the cookies) and her major role is the afternoon playgroup that will meet at her house. Being voted PTA President allows her to draw another experience card, which may result in her catching the mumps from the kids.

School Teacher-

To prepare to become a schoolteacher, the child is instructed to say toy boat three times real fast.

Animal Doctor-

The veterinarian is instructed to hop around the room like a frog. Now what veterinarian you know has to hop around like a frog to meet their requirements for the position?

The producers of the game included the "College Track." Maybe there is hope. Wrong! Instead of progressing, we are regressing. The college experience on the board directs a girl to: Fantasize about her teacher, to date a senior or to slow dance with her "main squeeze."

The game has been around since 1950, under the name, "Careers." What is most interesting is that it previously included careers in business, politics, and space exploration. At that time the game was being marketed to all children. Something to think about, hmmm. Well, do not stop here. Let's investigate further.

Picture this: A female child is playing with a toy and something breaks. Upon tearfully bringing it to her mother she hears the message, "Take it to daddy, he can fix it." The message-received results in statements such as the one by super model Beverly Johnson who said, "Men see a problem and they want to fix it." Her comments included how rewarding it was to have him offer, even though she did not believe in his ability to solve the problem.

Ponder this: How many of you buy houses, kitchen sets, and mommy-to-be dolls for your female child? Yes, mommy-to-be dolls. The ad states, "Judy looks like a real mommy-to-be. Take off her tummy and there's the baby." It retails for $19.95 plus shipping and receiving, (but of course you know that if you bought one). Get this; it is marketed for ages 3 and up. How much stronger does the message have to be? The ad also states the person ordering should allow 6-8 weeks for delivery. Why not make it realistic? Why not 9 months?

These examples further illustrate the lack of training a female receives on "being out there on her own" or even thinking about it.

24

Girls are socialized to expect few alternatives to being someone's wife. Historic research demonstrates that no society prepares women to be on their own. In Western society, the females adopt the language that gives you the clues that she believes the message. Mateless and dateless spells disaster, within the subconscious and society. When getting together with girlfriends you hear phrases like, "Here it is Saturday night and I'm out with women. I need to get a life," translation: I need a *man*. The resulting equation? Man + Woman = Life.

THE ASSIMILATION PROCESS

In marriage, women are frequently referred to as "my better half." Giving concessions for the fact that they did say "better" half, does that not indicate there is incompleteness? The phrase often heard within the traditional marriage ceremony is, "And the two shall become one."

Which one do they become? Is there an instant oneness, a melting into each other? He becomes she or she becomes he? You may be responding, "Oh come on now, be real, it doesn't mean that." The majority recognizes the phrase indicates a spiritual merging. Mathematically speaking does not $1+1 = 2$? Though the reference has its origin in the spiritual realm, it is commonly accepted that she becomes he. She accepts his name and derives her status in society from him.

Clergy, in times past, completed the marriage ceremony with, "I now pronounce you man and wife." Most recently some clergy and/or the couples have selected to change the phrase, to appropriately reflect the change in both individuals. The phrase is sometimes currently "I now pronounce you husband and wife." Now the two complete persons, coming together, make up something that could never have been had they remained apart. Mathematically speaking the results would still remain $1+1= 2$. This is not to say that two people, after getting to know each other, do not begin to think in similar patterns or finish each other's sentence. It is

25

acknowledged this can occur over a period of time when two people are in sync with each other and harmony develops.

The act of submission should be a voluntary act of your will, not as sometimes happens, a manipulative tool in the hands of the inexperienced, inept apprentice.

The socialization and assimilation process continues its effect in marriage with support from the "submission" theory. The moment women marry, they are expected to become selfless. Women are taught that a successful marriage is based largely on the willingness of the wife to adopt a submissive attitude. Previously, marriage vows supported the idea when women were required to repeat the words, "To love, honor, and obey." The obvious omission of the word "obey" in the vows repeated by the male made the implication clear. Wives are to submit. To many, the words mean to be less than or beneath the male personage, requiring self-denying behavior. Though the biblical command supports the need for a woman to obey, the text has often been used as a tool to put women in their place. A scripture, most often quoted by men, is I Peter 3:1, "In the same way, you wives, be submissive to your own husbands so that even if any of them are disobedient to the word they may be won without a word by the behavior of their wives."

This scripture has even been quoted to me by a wife, in a physically abusive marriage, as the justification for staying.

In exploring the theory of submission, the following chapter is presented with a hope. It is the hope that, with a heightened awareness of the dynamics of a relationship, one will not have to experience a *loss of self.*

LOSS OF SELF

What does it really mean to "submit?" Does it mean one *must* give up self for the relationship? To become a "silent" partner? Synonyms for the word "submit" can include: surrender, defer, relinquish, bow, comply, and obey. Does to obey mean the same as to submit?

26

It is no wonder women have the perception that one must give up self to meet another's needs. The truth is, the submission theory has gotten bad criticism based on a misinterpretation of its purpose. The misinterpretation has contributed to the enslavement of women. Dr. Tony Evans, an urban Pastor of the Evangelical Church, stated during a radio broadcast entitled, **_A Woman's Role in the Home_**, "To be subject does not mean to be enslaved."

Author Alice Walker wrote, "if a person is your friend, they will not seek to silence you or deny your right to grow." If women are required to lose their best qualities to keep the home stabilized, something is seriously wrong. Is it the system or the perception?

Traditionally, women have been socialized to believe they need a man for financial security, emotional stability, and social status. The idea of becoming Mrs. so-and-so to gain entrance into the social circle has been an accepted practice. In the past, a woman's sense of identity and self-worth were derived from marriage.

On the surface, the psychological effect appears minimal but what is not seen is the adverse effect the giving up of one's self has on the self-esteem. An anonymous writer stated, "No individual in a love relationship *"should feel"* that they have to give up an essential part of themselves to make it work."

Who said, **_you_**, the aforementioned individual, have to? Let's face it. You do not. The operative word in the statement is "I feel." Through societal pressure and stereotyping, you are made to "feel" that you must give up and give in to get along.

▲   So, why does it happen?

When did you begin to discount, devalue and disown your own thoughts, feelings and ideas?

How have these subconscious thought patterns formed in your life?

Who was responsible for the messages?

27

How did you develop into someone that feels manipulated by the masses? *Who's pulling your strings*?

WHO'S PULLING YOUR STRINGS?

Ever feel as if you are being pulled in a million directions at the same time? Does it feel as if everyone wants a piece of you and you're left feeling all used up, with little time for self? Do you constantly feel guilty for the number of long hours you work and even when you finally relax? Is that a **yes?** Most of you are internally yelling, "Yes, been there, done that, still doing it." Perhaps a few responded with the question, "What is wrong with that? I am a wife/girlfriend, mother, sister, employee, community activist, church member, delivery person and chauffeur for my children, just to name a few. I am supposed to do what I do." The latter retort reflects the sentiments of a popular television commercial.

You may remember the words of the jingle. It said, "I can bring home the bacon, fry it up in a pan and never let you forget you're a man." Again the question, what is wrong with that?

When you get a moment, reflect on your activities of the day. How much of it did you want to do or enjoy doing? (Take out a pencil and pen and do the work.)

No, don't respond with, "Who said I am supposed to enjoy it?"

When describing your activities, what "controlling" words did you use? Did you answer with,

This is just what I have to do...

Should do...

Supposed to...

Must...

28

Consider this:

▲ How and when did you evolve into someone who responds to everyone else's needs to the detriment of your own?

What factors contributed to your feeling like a marionette whose strings are being pulled and controlled by someone else, anyone else or everyone else?

When did you become powerless to control the activities of your life? To whom did you give the power?

When did you begin to devalue, discount, dismiss, and disown your feelings and needs?

When did you become the victim? Always giving in and giving it up to others, never placing self as number *one*?

Just when did you lose control and why? A well-known popular song tells us,

Life is a beautiful thing

As long as I hold the string

I'd be a silly so and so

If I should ever let it go

I say the process happened so gradually, you did not realize what was taking place until you were knee deep in it. Now, even you are convinced this is what you want for yourself and you actually enjoy being pulled apart at the seams. The results? *A Professional People Pleaser.* Someone once said, "We learn to smile to please rather than when pleased."

The innate desire to please speaks to your need to nurture and feel needed. As a consequence, you lie discarded in a corner, like little Suzy's rag doll, torn and shattered, waiting for the next opportunity to be used.

In light of the earlier questions, maybe an illustration would be helpful. The following scenario demonstrates the gradual descent of self within a relationship.

You meet someone new. You want to please. The individual asks you to go out to a movie. Even though you hate going to the movies, you consent to go. During this new relationship, he remarks that he does not believe you need makeup. "You're beautiful without it," he says. So what happens? You are flattered, of course, and begin to wear less or no makeup at all (at least when you are with him). He compliments you on how good you look in blue, his favorite color, and what happens? Your wardrobe tends to become expanded versions of blue. You go out with him to a social event. He steps away momentarily and a good-looking gentleman walks over and begins a casual conversation. Your body language indicates, to on-lookers, that you are enjoying the conversation. Your head is tilted to the side, you are smiling and occasional laughter interrupts the flow of conversation. Your partner returns and your new acquaintance quickly makes an exit. Your partner begins his interrogation: Who was he? What were you talking about? Why did he come over to talk to you? Did you initiate the advance by making eye contact? Clearly not satisfied with your answers or lack of answers, the discussion escalates. Soon, it is a full-blown, knockdown, drag-out fight.

If the relationship continues, how do you believe you will respond if a similar situation occurs? Undoubtedly, your response would tend to be less friendly, less outgoing, and quickly end any conversations with the male gender, before it even begins. You change and conform to please your mate. You find you are regularly going to the movies, not wearing any makeup and wearing more blue. Unquestionably, you are not responding socially, to those you encounter, with your bubbly God-given personality. The outcome of your desire to please ends in your becoming less than who you are.

Emptiness becomes your constant companion. You withdraw and your world becomes narrower. You give up lifelong friends (he does not like them) and you suspend your favorite pastime (he will miss you while you are gone). You systematically teach yourself to suppress and deny your feelings.

The effect is mental imprisonment. Not being allowed to say what you feel results in your finding other ways to express yourself. This is a tragic misuse of the brief time you have been given. You learn to push your own needs aside, forcing them deep into the subconscious, where they remain submerged. You feel as if the joy of life has been sucked out of you. Your frequent angry or tearful outbursts pushes people farther away, preventing anyone from knowing the real you.

The actions described in the previous scenario in and of them selves are not negative requests. There is nothing inherently wrong with going to the movies or wearing blue for your mate. Couples often compromise or defer their individual likes and dislikes in preference of the other. It is legitimate and valid to attempt to make concessions to please your mate. It becomes a problem when your whole wardrobe is excessively blue and you don't even like blue.

Do you know the ironic conclusion of this script? The individual for whom you changed, one day, looks at you and says, "I don't love you anymore. You're not the person I fell in love with. I'm not happy. You've changed." After the sting of his words and the numbing shock wears off, you hurl attitude filled words.

You say, "You're right, I changed. I changed for you. I thought you loved me."

He responds, "What's love got to do with it?" Somewhere deep inside, you realize that what he is saying is true. The *you* he fell in love with *is* no longer there and you never realized when she left. The process was so gradual you never saw it coming nor realized it had happened.

For a point of illustration, let's say a couple reaches the altar and one of the partners turns to the other. The one says to the other, "I am going to make your life a living *hell*." Now do you suppose they would marry? No, because upon hearing that statement the other partner would walk away. However, five years down the line, the couple wakes up and realizes their relationship **is a** living *hell.* They cannot understand how or when it happened. It was a gradual

31

process. Slow and steady. An older man at a nursing home described it when he said, "The trouble with life is, it's so daily."

Ever ask yourself the questions?

Why did I fall for that?

Why am I so gullible?

Why did I agree with the program?

When he suggested that I ... Why did I not recognize, react, and rebel?

There are many theories and patterns of thought that, in summary, lead one back to where it all began: the beginning.

In the beginning, as a baby you were fearfully and wonderfully made. The scriptures proclaim, "For you created my inmost being; you knit me together in my mother's womb." I praise you because I am fearfully and wonderfully made" (Psalms 139:13).

In your purest form you were free. Free of the ability to prejudge the individual that held you up and attempted to make you laugh. You simply laughed as an automatic response to the stimuli. You were innately born with only two fears, that of falling and of loud noises. All other fears were a result of learned behaviors. As an infant, you knew what you liked and did not like. You had no difficulty vocalizing your feelings.

When you were not satisfied, the entire household knew it and responded. You were full of ambition and your ability to achieve was unlimited.

Again the questions:

▲ What happened? What happened to the potential? What changed the self-centered *"me"* child into the **"we"** focused individual, finally into the *"thee"* people pleaser you now see in the mirror?

32

Are you now saying, "Enough with the questions. I need answers? What do I do now to stop people from playing on my emotions?"

Wait! Before further explanation, take a moment to reflect. On a piece of paper, using general terms, describe a situation in which you know someone is pulling your strings. Be it subtle or overt, you feel their manipulative control.

▲   What are some of the examples?

How do you respond to unreasonable demands? Be it from children, grandchildren, employer?

Do you respond with an attitude of helpless and hopelessness?

What emotions caused you to be vulnerable?

What were the underlying issues?

Who are the manipulators?

Who in your environment knows all too well how to trigger a flood of emotions?

What are your hot button issues, that when pushed, send you into a blind rage of emotions?

Continuing the explanation, let's return to your beginning as an infant, with your boundless energy to discover the key to the trap.

As you attempted to grow and develop, the socialization process continued. In the early stages of your development, you learned to mirror those within your immediate environment.

The primary influences included parent(s), grandparents, and siblings. As you grew, your environment expanded to include teachers, guidance counselors, clergy, neighbors, peers, other friends, and family.

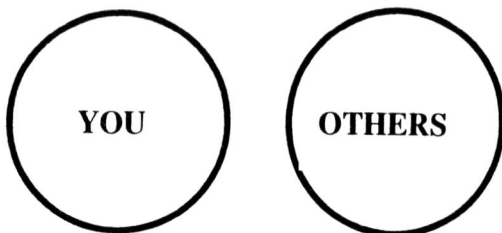

For the most part, individuals in your immediate environment were responsible for your development. They were to teach you right from wrong. They were liable for the development of your belief system, values, and how to conduct yourself appropriately (within societal norms). "But," you ask, "how does this explanation affect my present? Where is the problem?"

To answer the questions, let's make a closer examination of the individuals within your sphere of influence.

PARENTS

Though parent(s) are the principal players in influencing the outcome of your involvement, as a child, you failed to realize or recognize that your parent(s) were wounded. Through their own developmental process they too experienced hurt, anguish, and trouble. This generalized assumption is based on the statistical information that 98% of the population grew up in dysfunctional family systems.

As a child, you did not recognize the deep pain being experienced by your parent(s). You were probably intensely aware of the pain your parent(s) were inflicting on you, but their pain? Yes and their own hurts resulted in feelings of inadequacy, creating a cycle of excessive neediness. Bare in mind, your parents did not have access to the wealth of information on parenting available today. Information on how to respond to life was passed on from generation to generation.

The excess baggage being carried by the parent(s), the negative internal pressure, was projected subconsciously onto you, the child. You, in turn, felt the negative but did not understand the

34

source of the discomfort. You falsely assumed that if the family was not functioning, as it should, it must be "me." After all, unless the dysfunction is a major disruption within the family, a child does not look at the parent with an accusatory eye.

A child subconsciously looks to the parent for definition of self and for answers to how to behave appropriately within the context of society. A child learns early what behaviors are rewarded and praised and which are negatively received.

As the child, you begin to understand rather quickly what you better not say and whom you had better not say it to. Even though the emotions you felt were deeply experienced, they were not expressed. Perhaps you remember a similar incident when you stormed into the house and announced that you "Hated Aunt Susie (especially if she is your mom's sister")." You were met with an immediate response, "You do not hate Aunt Susie and do not let me ever hear you say that again." So you learned not to say it and you pondered the inner conflict. Your inner voice said, "I know I hate Aunt Susie but my mother says I don't."

Maybe you laughed aloud in church at something you felt was pretty hilarious. When you did, you were pinched and told, "That's not funny." You thought it was. To challenge is to be labeled a rebel, so you learned to become content with others making your decisions. You became afraid to say, "I do not like it when you...."

The majority of people, including the baby boomers, were raised during the era of "children should be seen and not heard."

In contrast to the present generation that freely expresses their feelings, you quietly became what others shaped you to be, although God only knows who and what you were destined to be. "One is born with a mass of expectations, a mass of other people's ideas—and you have to work through it all," as quoted by Mel Gussow in the N. Y. Times Book Review.

Throughout the process, what subconscious message did you receive and believe? You internally accepted that you couldn't trust your own feelings. Others' perceptions became your realities. You gave up control and became what others said you are. You lost your center and your identity. As you grew, the sphere of "Other's" influence increased.

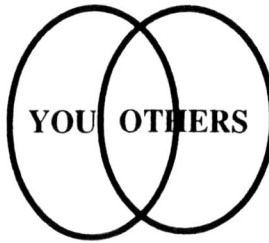

The results? You no longer listen to your inner voice because you believe it cannot be trusted. The larger the list, the more you feel inwardly victimized and powerless to take control. Over time, the effect is less and less of you and more of others reflected in you. Research compiled by Jakie DeFazio, president of the American Association of University Women indicates that by the time a young girl reaches her 15th birthday, her interests are likely to be narrowly defined and far less diverse (Plain Dealer article, November 30, 1996).

Though the diminishing of self also occurs in boys, it has been concluded that it is to a lesser degree and often temporary. And so it goes. The female child learns to be feminine, lovable, and to seek validation for her feelings and opinions. She learns to perfect the same characteristics that will, as an adult, make her vulnerable and susceptible to abuse. Her motivators become:

Fear of rejection

Fear of disapproval

(Motivated by the need to be liked)

Fear of the loss of love

The learned behaviors from childhood are carried into adulthood, carefully protected and maintained. Those who have a strong interest in controlling her behavior will use her fears. Low self-esteem will keep her in a place where she will continually compromise her integrity.

Reading the above information may prompt you to decide, "I want to restore, recapture, and get back what I lost. I want to take back control of my destiny." Your decision may involve going back to school or re-starting your career.

▲ What will happen when you decide to change? What will occur when you decide to grow toward the person you innately sense you were created to be?
How will the controllers react to change?

Be prepared. The path you choose will not be an easy one. If the controller is satisfied with the situation, the way it is, he will fight the change. Your level of commitment to regain self will either make or break the relationship. Your decision will be difficult to maintain but you must be persistently logical and confident in your need for change.

The conflicts that arise as a result can cause you to want to retreat back to the way things were, even though you were not happy. The subconscious is often satisfied with a known Hell over what is unknown. With the passing of time, the thoughts that say, "Maybe if I...then he...." begins to look more appealing than the present. Your memory replays the good times minus the hurtful ones. If by chance you succumb to the internal pressure (the manipulator's best tool) then you again do so to the detriment of self. In the wise words of Martin Luther King, Jr., "Life begins to end, the moment we become silent about things that matter."

So, "what is the answer?" you ask. "What do I do now to stop people from playing on my emotions? How do I stop merely existing and start living?"

If you have given serious consideration to the dilemma described above, can you allow yourself to admit the place you are in does not feel good?

When your identity is defined by others, the decisions you make are based on their values rather than your own. Until you take responsibility and discover why you do what you do, you will continue to do what you do not want done. The answer requires a

RENEWED COMMITMENT TO SELF.

The difficult task is to try to take charge of your life without completing the first step:

The Foundation.

A foundation can only be established through introspection. It requires you to take time to sit down, look into self, and evaluate your present through your past. "Well," you say, "That is what I am talking about. I do not have time for self." Then put this book down until you do.

Still here? Then let's proceed.

By regaining control, you will out maneuver the manipulators. Whether they are 3 or 33 years old, male, and female, friend, or foe, your decisions will be your own. You will gain confidence in your own value and become a self-empowered, productive human being.

Conclude to never let anyone, nothing (not a thing) define who you are. A powerful woman in history, Eleanor Roosevelt expressed, "I think somehow we learn who we really are and then live with that decision." From whom do we learn? Whose decision and definition do we live by? Do we really learn who we are?

Author Marianne Williams' words reflect that we have forgotten the role we were originally assigned to play. The author wrote, "We have lost the key to our own house. ...We must find the key."

How have I come to my conclusions? What research or statistics support the above illustration? Is it fiction or nonfiction? What documentation is there to uphold the theory? This chapter is a descriptor of a page from life. Its life application is not only representative of countless women but the story is my own.

My decision to terminate my marriage of 23 years came when I realized, I no longer desired to give up the essence of me for another. Having married at an early age, with the developmental process still incomplete, I lacked the foundation of a strong self-esteem. During my formative years, my growth process continued to be influenced by another. The person that has limited confidence in self all too often allows someone else to run his or her life. My lack of belief in self allowed for the acceptance and endurance of physical and verbal abuse. Once the demeaning behaviors and attacks on self were permitted, it became an accepted way of life. A sad facial expression became my countenance.

After many years of denial, crises created the urgent need to take a look at the situation and my role in it. It was to begin asking myself the hard questions:

> What demands were being made that did not allow me to be me?

> What was occurring in the relationship that caused me to feel badly about the person I was?

> How was I contributing to its continuation by blaming myself and taking responsibility for his irrational behavior?

> How long could I, or would I, continue to allow pleasing him to dominate my life?

> What affect were my thinking patterns having on the relationship?

The dangerous thinking pattern was in thinking

He would be nice if only I would

Or

If I would change this

Or

It was internalizing and accepting responsibility for how he chose to act. The internal guilt said, "I must be doing something wrong."

As awareness of self occurred, the difficult task became how to take charge of my life, while maintaining the relationship? It soon became evident that it was not only a difficult task but also an impossible one. The instinct for self-preservation and the need to survive overcame my fears of living outside the relationship. The need to rediscover *"me"* became the driving force, the motivator, which pushed me deeper into the search for the lost self.

Answering the hard questions only began the process of change. After years of evaluation, hard work, self-discovery, and recovery, the end result is an ability to educate others. The results are an increased awareness of what influences our outcome, why we do what we do, and how to create positive results. It is my own experience that helps me to bring women from where I have been to a place where healing and growth can occur. It is to be able to finally say,

"I run this."

Until one sits down and evaluates her individual happiness quotient, whether in a married state or not, she will continually allow others to control, while living a non-productive, unfulfilled existence.

During a survey conducted by IMJ ReeSources, couples married an average 40 - 50 years were asked questions regarding the giving up of self for the marriage. Individuals generally reported the feeling of having given up too much. To further emphasize the point, the respondents answered differently when separated from their partners than when together. Couples exhibited an inability to speak up and express their feelings to their spouse. They learned to privately complain and continue the cycle. All in the name of love or stability. ***What's love got to do with it?***

CHAPTER 3

<u>WHAT'S LOVE GOT TO DO WITH IT?</u>

In times past, couples married, and stayed married, for a hundred different external reasons. The reasons range from the desire for a family to wanting to avoid fornication. Love had little to do with it. Granted, love can come with time but most marriages were consummated for a variety of reasons. When asked why did you marry, most respond, "I fell in love." An anonymous author wrote, "There is no difference between a wise man and a fool when they fall in love." The term "fell in love" has always personally caused internal confusion and created questions.

Does not the phrase "to fall" mean to come from a high place to a lower place? To lose control? Sort of like falling into a well?

Should not the phrase be, I am in love, reflecting the status of the relationship? Or "was" in love maybe? Just something to make you go, hmmm.

ROMANTIC LOVE (Emotional)

Romantic love is to *fall* in love first and then try to look for reasons. Phrases frequently used, after the romanticism has worn off in the relationship include:

"I know you tried to tell me. I just could not see his faults"

"I chose not to look at his problems"
"I just closed my eyes and hoped it would be different"
"I must have been blind not to see"

Being in love is often a fantasy with no reality base. It has been said, "Love is the triumph of imagination over intelligence." Words of the song, "What's Love Got To Do With It," sung by

Tina Turner in the movie of the same name, imply that love is just a second-hand emotion.

What might the first emotion be?

Is it a reaction to a long-held fantasy or is it a prelude to sex?

Is it romantic love, addictive love or true committed love?

Have the individuals come together out of frustration or desperation, with each having a frantic need to cling to another person?

It has been said, "Love is an emotion that can be classified as both negative and positive. It can cause great joy and pain."

Romantic love, when it occurs, administers its anesthesia causing the individual under its spell, to be swept away into the romanticism of the new relationship.

Madagascar proverb warns, "Don't be so much in love that you can't tell when the rain comes."

Individuals caught up in the romantic feeling of love often do not take the necessary time to get to know each other. The first stage of romantic love emphasizes the physical and heightens the euphoria, without the necessary spiritual connectedness. Romantic love does not let you know the other person. The greatest fantasy on earth is the idea that you will have someone in your life who will always, forever trigger that special feeling in you. The truth is, the quick, exciting feelings of love fade for a more realistic, less glamorous but sustaining emotions. Let's face it, it must or lovers would never get anything done. Romantic love based on passion will have its highs and lows. With maturity, the insatiable passion for each other turns into a comfortable, satisfying relationship. Comfort accompanies wild passion. A healthy relationship knows how to balance love, sex, and life.

ADDICTIVE LOVE (Immature)

Addictive love says, "I come together with you to get something from you." This form of love says, "I love you because I need you."

An example of immature love comes from an illustration presented in a Sunday morning sermon by Pastor L. Boone. The illustration asks you to picture yourself with a bottle of pop in your hand. Perhaps it's an extremely hot day and you remark, "I love this Pepsi Cola." What does your statement mean? Will your love for the ice cold bottle of pop you hold in your hand, prompt you to do anything for that pop? Sounds absurd, doesn't it? Of course, you have no intentions of doing anything *for* the bottle of pop except drinking it. When you finish emptying it of its substance, you will discard the container. The sermon's objective was to create the understanding that Immature Love only seeks for what is fulfilling to the individual's needs.

Unfortunately, just as in the illustration, Immature Love will discard the object (the person) of their affection when they no longer serve their usefulness. You have heard the words of sister girlfriend that said, "Yeah, girl, as long as he is paying my rent, I'll keep him until ALL his money's spent." Immature Love does not ask, "What can I do for you, only what's in it for me?"

In contrast, Mature love says, "I need you because I love you."

In addictive love, a separate sense of self becomes secondary to the relationship. "If love means that one person absorbs the other, then no real relationship exists any more." (anonymous)

They (the couple) are bound by an excessive neediness. The couple or individual's world becomes narrower over time, with activities that once were important to the individual, falling aside. This often includes family and friends.

In addictive love, couples become intertwined, wrapped up in each other, creating a strained relationship. The relationship is often characterized by the couple's inability to identify where one

45

partner ends and the other begins. The relationship becomes limiting versus liberating. So limiting that they become toxic, from breathing their own stale air. The stifling effect keeps one or both partners from doing the things they want to do. They develop a codependent alliance, losing their emotional perspective. They lose themselves inside the relationship. In an article in the December issue (Complete Woman/1995), Dr. Doreen Virtue declared, "If there's more unfulfillment than joy in your relationship, something needs to change!"

A devastating blow occurs when one partner, feeling suffocated, moves toward independence. The individual expresses their intentions by announcing that he/she is "leaving on the midnight train to Georgia." Joan Crawford once called love a fire. She said could never tell whether it would warm your hearth or burn down your house."

TRUE LOVE

True committed love is the fulfillment of a relationship of two people coming together to share a lifetime of love. It is to come together out of completeness. It is not needing anything from the other, yet having the possibility of generously choosing to give and to be there. When in a relationship that is functioning correctly, "I can see what I see and say what I see." It is two people standing side by side, looking inward and outward at the same time.

A quotation from the booklet, *God's Little Instruction Book on Love*, says, "Love does not consist in gazing at each other but in looking together in the same direction."

It is not becoming enmeshed or entangled by love or so entrapped you cannot get out. Some would say that love is just a feeling. So what happens when you do not feel loved, does it cease to exist?

A cousin, Pastor Joseph Garlington related an experience he had one morning. After awakening Pastor Joseph turned to his wife, Barbara, and said, "Honey, I don't feel married." Barbara turned over and replied, "See that ring on your finger? You are." True love is to make a conscious choice, a sacrifice. It

is not based on feelings. A tremendous amount of energy must go into this kind of love, to be loving and to be loved.

Motivational speaker and author of, *Loved, Loving and Being Loved*, Semia Bray outlines the results of true love. It is enduring and it does not always exhibit itself in a grandiose manner. It displays itself often in quiet action as simple as:

Running your bath water in anticipation of your arrival
Or
Opening the front door before you can place the key in the door
Or
Slipping off and unobtrusively putting gas in your car, so you will not have to stop on your way to work in the morning.

A couple attending premarital counseling was asked by their minister, "Do you need each other?" Gazing lovingly into each other's eye, they answered what they thought was the appropriate answer, "Yes." The minister then proceeded to help them explore their level of neediness and to understand coming together out of desire versus need. True love is born out of an urge to fulfill oneself through another.

The difficulty occurs when one is absorbed completely by the other. Inner turmoil exists when one seeks to lose self, to become one, but in contrast senses the need to maintain separateness.

After serious introspection, the couple in the a fore mention counseling session, may reach some startling conclusions. They may come to realize they need to first have a relationship with themselves before coming together with another.

The questions become, "How can we be for each other if we are not first for ourselves?" This insight may cause them to discover they have been ***Looking for love in all the wrong places***

LOOKING FOR LOVE IN ALL THE WRONG PLACES

THE SEDUCTION

PICTURE THIS:

You arrive at a social event and after a few minutes of circulation, your eyes spot someone across the room. Your eyes connect, for a few moments, with the eyes of an incredibly good looking man. You watch with passion-filled eyes as he makes his way through the crowd, passing several women, until he is standing next to you. As he moves still closer, the scent of his Hugo Boss cologne absolutely drives you crazy with desire. It is as if a magnetic field was pulling you to him. His eyes are mentally undressing you but you do not mind because you can see the enviable look on other women's faces. You conclude that any one of them would jump at the opportunity to wake up the next morning in his arms. During the intimate conversation that ensues you realize. "He's actually listening to me." The pickup line comes, "Let's leave and go somewhere private so I can get to know you better." Flattered at being selected, chosen from the crowd, you fall *hook*, *line* and *sinker*.

THE HOOK

After only a few days into the relationship, you would do anything to keep him. The relationship has now moved into the make-believe stage. You begin wanting to spend every minute with him. You organize your day around his phone calls and the anticipation of hearing his voice. You rush home or stay home and wait, wait, wait. Afraid of jeopardizing the new relationship, you will do whatever it takes to keep him. Your technique includes the enticement of sex, though this will only appeal to the man who goes through life with his fly open. You are afraid to show who you really are for fear that he will request his walking papers. So,

48

you become what you think he wants you to be. You become intensely involved in how he makes you feel rather than who he is.

Sound familiar? The truth is many women become helplessly and hopelessly hooked on the feeling of romance. More in love with the feeling of "being in love" than the experience of loving. The new relationship is so seductive it catches you on the blind side. You are seduced by the thought that "he needs me and I need to be needed." The relationship has now entered the codependent stage. The fallacy here is to come to the conclusion that since he makes me feel wonderful, he must be wonderful. Wrong. You have just experienced Prince Charming.

The name, Prince Charming, is a derivative of the word, "charm," meaning he is really attractive. His technique is to be charming in the beginning and he will do almost anything initially to get you. This type of individual knows what to do, when to do it, and where. He opens doors, tells you how incredibly beautiful you are and .He gets you talking. The more you talk, the more information he has, to know how to please you. Problem? Yes, his only purpose is to use the information until you are helplessly and hopelessly hooked. **And** you believe it is **Magic**. Misunderstood, the feeling of love, can cause you to marry a real jerk. You become attracted to the window dressing and do not stop to consider his character. When the sparks ignite, creating a flame of passion, you reach for an apron. You're ready to turn "Mr. Magic" into the ideal "Mr. Stay-at-home-every-night husband." However, when you stop to think about it, does interest mean long-term commitment?

JUST WHO IS HE ANYWAY?

Take this questionnaire before you begin reading this chapter.

▲ Is there someone in your life that fits the "Prince Charming" description?
Just who is he anyway?

49

Who is he when you strip away the window dressing?

What do you see?

What is beneath the surface?

Is he honest or have you already detected lies?

Is he generous or an irresponsible spender?

Does he pay his bills?

Does he keep his word?

Can you count on him to be there?

What are his thoughts on family? Commitment?

When he walks into the room, does your body react before your mind engages?

How does he respond when troubles crowd and press?

Is there a Dr. Jekyll/Mr. Hyde personality lurking inside? A dark side?

What are his political views?

What are his sexual patterns?

Do you really believe he will reveal all of his sexual encounters to you or even should he?

What did you learn? What did you see when you looked deeper?

If the majority of your responses were negative or "I do not know" then it is time to put on the brakes. There appears to be a lot you need to learn about the man that you propose to love. Martin Luther King Jr. once said, "It is impossible to unsee what you have seen."

When you choose to look deeper, to face the nagging inner fears of what you may discover, you deflate the fantasy's obsessive power. Fantasies rarely hold up to close scrutiny. The more madly in love you are, the longer you should take to get to know the object of your affection. Work to discover his negative traits. "But I am in love, I don't need to.." Yes, it has been said, "Love is blind but only by choice."

It is time to take the blinders off and realistically assess the relationship. It is important to appraise the principles by which he operates:

Appraise his value and belief system.
What are the dynamics of his family?
Is there a strong line of communication? How does he respond to his mother, sister? I know you have heard that one before.

When faced with the realities of a relationship, many women tend to not see the obvious. Take, for example, a woman who enters a relationship with a man who has previously married three times. She feels lucky to be number four and does not even consider the contributing factors to his failed relationships. What part did he play? He was not at fault, right? Right thinking patterns become eschewed. When the same individual (living the above scenario) watches a talk show, she has sound advice for all the panelist being evaluated. Sometimes even the show's guest panelist has advice for the others seated on the stage but does not have a clue about her own situation.

Another for instance:

Your family is small and intimate. You enjoy frequent get together's (weekly or monthly) and regularly scheduled Holiday celebrations as a family. He comes from a large family and you assume that means a lot of close family interactions. Good fit? Not! You have assumed too much. Only as time passes do you discover he does not communicate with his family and he resents the closeness of yours. Is the picture becoming clearer?

Perhaps you are responding with, "Why do I have to know all that? I just want to sleep with him one night." Watch out! Again your assumptions lead you to believe there will be no strings attached to the object of the one-night stand. Just slam, bam, and thank you ma am. Only the unseen can reveal immediately what you will later discover. To walk away from a one-night stand is like stumbling into the transparent threads of a spider web. Though it appears there are no strings attached, silently the web has been weaved. The entanglement of the trap becomes only apparent with the passing of time.

One day when you wake up from the fairy tale gone sour, you realize your response had nothing to do with love. Your conditioned responses were based largely on your desire to be with someone. You question his actions by asking, "But you said you loved me?" His words echo hard into your head, sending daggers into your heart. "Yes, I said I loved you and you dropped your panties. Its called salesmanship." (Dialogue from a salesman, Tales of the Crypt.) Only through introspection, do you ascertain, that not only do you *not know who he is* but you do *not know who you are*. Ask yourself: Are you susceptible to Prince Charming because you are afraid of being alone?

Take a moment to ponder: Does **being** **alone** mean **being lonely**?

ALONE OR LONELY: Which are you?

Visit any watering hole where women gather and somewhere, at any given time, you will hear a member of the group vocalizing her inner fears. The words expressed usually follow the pattern that says, "I've never been without a man. I don't know what I'd do if I didn't have one. I guess I'm lucky."

A *woman* without a *man*. An interesting phenomenon.

What is a woman like, who does not have a man? You would answer, "It depends on the woman." Your response would be a correct one. One individual can be outside a relationship, but not feel lonely. For another, it can be devastating. Henry David Thoreau, who lived alone for almost two years at Walden Pond, wrote of how much he enjoyed privacy in Walden. ..Why should I feel lonely? ..To be in company, even with the best, is soon wearisome and dissipating. I love to be alone." Another can feel that to be with a man is like being attached to a lung machine. Her expressions create the thought that, if he leaves, she will die. Remember the song by Toni Braxton, *"I'll never breathe again?"* The latter individual would experience loneliness in their aloneness. This is not to say that everyone does not experience loneliness from time to time yet for the healthy individual it is not a permanent condition. The healthy individual seeks to understand. The unhealthy individual's thought pattern says, "I cannot be happy unless I am with someone". This individual believes happiness to be outside herself, the responsibility of someone else. Beatrice Berry quoted, during a presentation in Cleveland, Ohio, "Unless we are willing to have no mate, we will have a toxic mate."

Beatrice speaks to the fact that women are afraid to fly solo. Afraid to be alone. In the past, singleness as a lifestyle was not viewed as a desirable or positive recognizable way of life. To be single meant you were, as they say, between marriages. It was like being between jobs. The expectation was that you were seeking, but unfortunately had not found, your place amongst the married. This position brought unsolicited sympathy from misinformed and misguided friends. It took the Oprah Winfrey's and Beatrice Berry's of the world to legitimize singleness.

What causes the feeling of loneliness? What is at the core?

Is the status of aloneness by choice?

How does she cope with loneliness?

Women in business, who appear to be confident, to those within her sphere of influence in the business arena, are often wearing a mask. A change of scenery and her confidence disappears and she begins to second-guess herself. The fears become apparent and the facade disappears in the face of solitude. Women of professional status, that appear to have it all together, sometimes fall into the category that requires a man to make them feel whole. They reveal themselves to be women who need a man's approval and acceptance to feel validated. To fill the hole in the soul. They make statements that carry the message that women are validated by their husband. A study compiled by psychiatrist, David Burns, author of *Feeling Good*, reported in 1992, that there were 100 million lonely hearts.

An episode of the television series, "Living Single", aired November 2, 1995, accurately reflected the sentiments of the larger population of women. Listen to the conversation that took place:

Regine:

> Now look at us, manless. I may not have a man at the moment but it hasn't been that long since I had a date. Oh my God, it's been two months. It hasn't been "this" bad since the drought of 89' and that was only because I was visiting friends in Alabama and refused to go out with anyone named Baby Brother, Butter or Bookie.

An episode from the television series, "A Different World", related the following dialogue: "I am not lonely, I am alone. What is the difference? I don't know." Not understanding what motivates the fear causes the individual to continue living with a damaged ability to love. Simply going to bed *"alone"* can trigger the question, "Will I have to sleep alone for the rest of my life?"

If the above descriptor fits you ask yourself the question: Why do I feel lonely? The root of loneliness is in you, not in him. You have to be in a good relationship with yourself before you can be in a good relationship with a man. Anton Chekhov states, "If you are afraid of loneliness, do not marry."

When surveyed 9 of 10 women said marriage was better than living alone. It is the tenth woman who understands it is better to want what you do not have than to have what you do not want. My bout with loneliness occurred after marrying young (at 16 years of age), and discovering I had never had the opportunity to experience life without a man. Going from my father's house to my husband's house did not allow me that opportunity. While married, I learned to face the flip side of the question, "Will I have to sleep alone for the rest of my life?" to "Why do I feel so alone with a man sleeping beside me?

One's feeling of loneliness does not require a person to be isolated. I found that it was not only possible but probable that an individual can be lonely within the context of marriage. A person can live a lonely existence while surrounded with people including

54

husband, children and family. They are individuals who stay married out of habit, who no longer have a passion for love or life. Certainly a very sad existence. Their lives appear to be full yet the feeling of loneliness permeates. They are in relationships that concluded long before anyone made the decision to formally end it. The pattern then repeats itself. Unless the individuals evaluate their emotions during the reconstruction period, they will continue to not feel validated and repeat the same relationship pattern.

The difficulties increase when the female fails to realize a *man* can not fill the hole in the soul or the emptiness that drives the hunger. An emptiness that urges the hunger to be satisfied. The hole is a result of unfinished business. An emotional vacuum left by the unmet needs of childhood and or past experiences. Your parents, designed to be the first two lovers in your life, had 15 - 18 years to fill your love tank. The sum total of a person is the result of where they have been. The feeling of insecurity in a love relationship can be a consequence of a lack of unconditional love in childhood. The abandonment of a father, can cause the female child to be sensitive to rejection. For the female, the relationship with her father, or lack of it, can affect her adversely. This sensitivity carries over subconsciously into relationships and the female takes personal responsibility when her mate or first date does not call. Beatrice Berry stated, "If someone does not call after a first date, it says more about him than it does about me."

Clinical psychologist Diane Adile Kirschner, Ph.D. reports that women with high self esteem are able to stay on the dating treadmill for a longer period of time than women who look to others to foster their sense of self. Why? A high sense of self increases one's ability to be resilient. The ability to bounce back from the realities of rejection, while dating, is an essential survival technique.

A first date can increase the individual's self doubts based on her perception of how the date went. A female may wonder whether her date liked her enough to call again. If he does not call, her self-esteem suffers. She may give way to the fear of being alone and do something degrading to gain the desired attention. The feeling of stimulation each time she is victorious is its own reward. Yet the results can be the destruction and ruin of another relationship.

IN SEARCH OF LOVE?

HOW TO
GET IT
IF YOU WANT IT

CHAPTER 4

ARE THEY REALLY THAT BAD?

Women suffering from dating burnout have a familiar complaint. Where are all the good men? Are they married, gay or in jail? I guess it depends on your definition of good. *ARE MEN REALLY THAT BAD?*

The Roger Organization poll found growing numbers of women expressing sensitivity to sexism and unhappiness with men on many issues. In 1970 2/3's of the women polled described men as basically kind, gentle and thoughtful. Twenty years later in a new poll only half of the 3,000 surveyed agreed. (Associated Press)

A few years later in 1995, women attending workshops entitled, "A Good Man Is Hard To Find," described men in quite a different tone. The list of nouns and adjectives used included the following examples:

Ungrateful	Nasty	Liars	Lazy
Kind	Dogs	Self-centered	Diseased
Baffling	Inconsiderate	Babies	Caring
Understanding	Mean	Controlling	Jealous
Irresponsible	Cheats	Leeches	Impatient

With no guidance or prodding from the facilitator, women freely, spontaneously provided their description of men. Their phrases included kinder and gentler words, nonetheless, the majority caused men to appear to be inept, unprepared and the cause of the destruction of relationships. It appears that women innately blame men for what ails them. Women appear to blame men instinctually although it is a learned behavior. Case in point, even the terminology regularly used place men at the root of the problem. Look at some painful situations and the words associated with them.

MENopause

MENtal Illness

MENstruation

Guynecologist

HISterectomy

HIMorrhoids

Now quickly before this turns into a male bashing session (someone may say too late) answer the following questions:

What changed from the first group surveyed to the group of women attending the workshops in 1995?

What caused the disintegrating perception of men?

Have men actually become progressively worse with time?

What is the reason for the growing dissatisfaction with men?

Are they solely responsible for the state of   relationships? Is this really fair?

Again the question, . **are men really that bad?**

In conversations with women, when male bashing occurs, the females begin using various descriptors to speak to the man's character. Pot shots may even be aimed at parts of his anatomy. Although it may occur, as she is leaving a friend asks, "Where are you going?" Her response? "Out with one of them." It is amazing how frequently women berate men in conversation but seek to be constantly surrounded by their presence. Comedian Melony Camacho lamented during her stand-up comedy routine, "I used to want one to wine and dine me, now I want one that can take care of his own D_ _ _ self."

So again the question: **Are** men really that bad? Let's attempt to gain insight into a theory of what happened.

CHANGE

A man marries with fantasies in his head as to how things are going to be. Dr. Charles Swindoll, from his book, *Grace Awakening* describes the desire of every groom to marry a woman who is the perfect blend of Mother Teresa, Betty Crocker, Kristi Yamaguchi and Whitney Houston.

A man marries and he has a general idea of his expectations. He has lived with a female, his mother and/or sister, and he expects typical female behavior. Let's consider that in his household the female did the cooking, cleaning, raised the children and responded to the male's sexual needs upon demand. The female he marries, on the other hand, observed the stay-at-home behavior of her mother. After assessing the results of her mother's choice, she decides to give way to the societal pressure that encourages liberation from the life style of her mother. The economic condition of society now dictates a woman's need to work, so she is encouraged to do so. Often to the detriment of the home.

Contrary to popular belief, a 1993 Gallop Poll showed that 40% of the women surveyed believe the women's movement has made women's lives harder. Women began to feel the inner need to grow, to expand and to stretch. To reach her potential, the female decides to return to school to restart her career. It all sounds good, right? However, the difficulties begin when, along with her newfound freedom, she now expects the male "to assist with the housework and be supportive."

This does not imply there is any thing wrong with the request. Yet consider: The participation in the chores associated with housework was not what he expected or desired. Of the men surveyed, 52% felt equitable division of housework is the greatest cause of resentment.

Male response?

His statements include:

        I let you...(go to work, school, etc.)

        Now you expect...

The male begins having painful feelings about the change. Even men who are positive about the change also have intensely negative feelings that complicate relationships.

As women got full-time jobs and good paying jobs, men suppressed emotions that said, "I should be the sole bread winner." If a man grew up in a family system where the father was the sole breadwinner and the mother was a submissive, dependent homemaker, his emotions become deeply rooted through his experience.

His response to changing roles?

- The feeling of loss identity, sense of self
- Find it necessary to keep women down for the sake of their own ego
- Exhibit a lack of respect for women

He may begin to question

How do I relate? What is my role in the family? What are the expectations? Will I or can I measure up? Catch up?

According to Dr. Julia Hare, Executive Director of the Black Think Tank, "Men are constantly being told they cannot measure up. No matter how others view them, inside they feel inadequate and blame themselves."

The male continues to fight, making decisions that the female does not agree with. She does what she wants and the male eventually begins to emit the automatic, resigned response, "Do what you want, I don't care" or a less combative, patronizing, "Yes, Dear." Feeling a loss of self-identity, he may seek to regain control but he is not sure how to react. His reaction is to become deceptively passive. He may seek escape to cover his temporary pain with temporary solutions through drugs, food, work or sex.

Responding like the life has been beat out of him through societal pressures and the female's high expectations. Results? *A*

GOOD MAN becomes a wimp (women discard wimps) and goes underground.

The female response to the male's response?

Typically, she initially tries desperately to please her partner who is often angry, combative and intimidating. She may later counter with defensive behaviors, becoming domineering and aggressive.

An aggressive female will ultimately become overbearing, intimidating and too threatening. She robs the man of his masculine role. Eventually when a decision needs to be made, the male responds with lackadaisical frustration. The results may be a feeling (on the part of the female) of abandonment and rejection by the male. Daughters of dads who left. The ghost of a lost relationship with her father may be responsible for her present actions. After a few more futile attempts to effectively communicate her needs, the female resorts to subtle hints. Her recourse may include head games, open nagging and maniacal manipulation.

And the beat goes on and on and on......

The men in the relationships described above, become angry as the women challenge their power, further exposing them to the reality of their own powerlessness (as defined by society). We fear what we do not understand. Men, who feel powerless, often have a greater need to think of women as inferior, to strengthen their position. The angry male does not express the first emotion he is experiencing. It may include: the fear of losing his partner or the loss of power or control. He masks his true feelings, resulting in subtle and sometimes direct rebellion. He again tries to regain control.

Think about it:

▲ How do you react when you feel you have loss control of your children?

What do you do? Beat them?

Remember wrestling with a sibling as a child and being pinned down? The more they held you down, the more you

63

struggled to be freed. Thus the female or male's attempts to gain control is resisted. An anonymous writer once said, "What you resist, persist." Try to change a man, he resist. Think about how difficult it is to change yourself. Many women accept the well meaning advice of a popular love guru that says, "If you cannot change your man, exchange your man."

Bulletin news flash

<u>NO ONE CAN CHANGE ANYONE</u>

Considering the aforementioned statement, consider:

Can you live with the situation as it is now, not as you hope it might be? It might change or it might not and if it does change, it could get worse.

Ever notice how even the minister reminds you of the possibility during the traditional wedding vows when he says, "For better or for worse?" "Oh," but you protest loudly, "But it could get better." But you also still believe in fairy tales, do you not?

There is a story of a woman who was married to a tyrant, an egotistical maniac or so it goes. He believes a woman should be bare foot and pregnant all the time. And so she was. Her well meaning friends continually tried to tell her to get out of the situation. She would only reply, "It could get worse." One day and four children later, her husband left her for a younger woman. Her friends confronted her with the usual, "I told you so" and she only responded with, "It could be worse." They could not understand. How could it be worse? So they asked, "How could it possibly be worse? She answered, "He could come back."

If the other person needs changing to fit your social, economical ideal, you are in a relationship headed for trouble. Avoid trying to change or correct your partner's personal reality.

Your mate will have one of two reactions: To become defensive or withdrawn.

So, if you cannot change your man or exchange your man, does it mean you have to accept the man the way he is? What part of him will you accept? **Is a piece of man better than no man at all?**

IS A PIECE OF MAN BETTER THAN NO MAN AT ALL?

During previous seminar sessions, when asked the question, "Is a piece of a man better than no man at all?", the majority of women respond immediately with a resounding, "NO." A few women, after a moment of hesitation, laughingly reply, "It depends on which piece you are talking about." Still others answer unashamedly, "YES, I hate being alone. My momma always told me a half of loaf is better than no loaf at all." For those of you that say "NO" consider:

A friend calls you up and says, "I have got someone for you to meet." How do you respond? Are your first questions, what does he look like and what does he do? Men report the most frequently asked questions at social gatherings (after "what is your name) are, "What do you do and what do you drive?" A previous supervisor (who shall remain nameless in case he would like to use the line again) when asked the question, "What do you drive?" Answers, "A Yugo. You go catch the bus." Why not ask what his interests are? His response to the question will tell you what you have in common. Maybe you are saying, I need to know how much he makes so I can determine if he is established, disciplined and goal oriented. Will not his interest reveal that information. The answer requires listening skills.

Meditate for a moment on the following series of questions.

▲ What do you want in a man? For what are you looking? What features are important to you? What are your expectations and from where did they come?

65

When asked the previous questions, a majority state they have not given much thought to the type of man they would like. They can usually tell you what they do not want.

Take time to describe your ideal man. Go ahead and jot down a list of what you want and be specific in your description. Be as clear as you possibly can.

An excerpt taken from the VFW magazine describes a woman talking to her friends about her two beaus. She says, "If I could combine their qualities, I'd be the happiest person in the world. Ronald is rich, handsome and witty. Tony wants to marry me."

Attendees participating in workshops entitled, "A Good Man Is Hard To Find," when asked to complete the previous exercise, provided extensive profiles.

The following is a sample list of stereotypical characteristics. Women want men to be:

strong	macho	sexy	financially stable
caring	possessive	loyal	good looking
loving	humorous	happy	communicative
sweet	successful	gentle	
patient	unselfish	physical	
concerned	humble	romantic	
sensitive but not wimpy			

A diversity of ages in a group often reflects a difference in what they want in a man. The varied response between age groups supports the theory that what you would select at 17, you would not select at 35. Do your own survey. Ask young women under the age of 21, what they want in a man and then ask women 30 years and older. Compare their answers. How often were outside trappings selected over characteristics not so readily visible? Outside window dressing versus internal character?

As children grow, a picture develops in their mind of what a good relationship should look like. After finding a mate, the individual goes about creating that relationship without much

66

participation from their partner. The result is a relationship with themselves. Often, unconsciously, women choose a mate who repeats the wounding patterns of her childhood. The selected partner has the predominant character trait of the parent or dominant person in the female's childhood environment. Now remember before you prepare your rebuttal. The process is a subconscious action and is not a conscious choice.

Another close examination of the list of ideals often reveals that the characteristics desired are those predominantly displayed by the female gender. Yes, when the question was explored within a workshop setting, women acknowledged they want men to be more like them. This is not to say men do not possess classic feminine qualities (most will not admit it) but the norm is not to display them.

Evaluate your list and weigh this question: How can one man have all the characteristics you have listed? "Well," you say, "he does not have to have all of them." So the question becomes, with what will you be satisfied? Are you looking for a "PERFECT" man or a "REAL" man? If he does not have all the characteristics on your list, will that mean he is less than a man? or **A PIECE OF A MAN?**

Let's say you meet a man and he is:

Loving (responsive to your needs)
Responsible (watches your children when you need to go somewhere)
Ambitious (have big plans for the future)
Loyal (would not dream of speaking negatively of you in public) and
Outgoing (never met a stranger)

You get the idea. Does he sound like someone you want to be with? "But wait a minute," you reply, "no money? I'm looking for a man who is tall, dark and has some." Money has led many women to bed and kept them there. Even after a committed relationship goes bad, many will stay for the financial gain. Billy

Preston pinned a song in which the words reflect the serious thoughts of relationships and money. The words said, "Nothing from nothing leaves nothing and you got to have something if you want to be with me." Another sentiment says, "I don't want nothing broke in my house. No broke dishes, appliances and definitely no broke MAN."

Is this true of you? Before you loudly protest and say that ain't true, look around you. I would venture to say, you can probably find two or three women that agree. Someone once said, "Romance without finance is ignorance or a nuisance." I have heard women state emphatically, "I want my men to be like cheese cake. Very rich."

Imagine this:

You walk into a room and there are four men in the room. Through conversation, you discover three of the men are operating at an economic disadvantage. One appears to be financially secure and independently established. Whom would you approach in the interest of developing a serious relationship? Come on. Be real. Let's face it. How many can handle a brother not having finance? Men understand this all too well and express feeling the potential mate (date) will not accept what they have to offer.

So they lie. It is their rebuttal to their worth being measured by the size of their wallet. Their number one complaint is women who are status seekers. The woman who they perceive to be too materialistic. They state, "The minute we meet, they want to know where we work, how much we make and how many degrees we have." You know how the story goes. Man meets woman. Man has an annual salary of $17,000. Man and woman get emotionally involved. Woman runs out on man when another man enters the picture making $35,000.

Does this illustration place women in a bad light? Okay, let's soft pedal it. Instead of saying some women are looking for a man with a big wallet, perhaps it is more pleasant to say, a man with a "big heart."

So let's go deeper into the above scenario. What happens when you are working and he is not? Does the Golden Rule apply? He/she who has the gold, rules? Money = Power. This creates an internal struggle for the man who has been trained to be in control. The man that society expects or demands to be the bread winner. It takes a serious brother to handle his mate earning three times the amount that he makes. The majority will say when asked, "Hey, I can handle it. Bring it to me. I'm happy for her." Then you watch the relationship change.

Why the continued focus of the money issues of a relationship? Through conversations, it appears to be a reoccurring theme and one for serious consideration. Money is self-expression and has no morality in and of itself. How one feels about money will determine its value and influence within the relationship. It is important to begin with the truth of where you are. To realize what you need most can not be satisfied with money. An anonymous writer disagreed and stated, "The man that said money cannot buy happiness, does not know where to shop." Money has been found to bring pleasure but not peace. A house but not a home. It can buy people but not friends.

▲ Have you come to any conclusions?
What characteristics are important to you? Is intimacy or you synonymous with sex? As long as you are getting **it** and **it's good**, nothing else matters?
Is it purely sexual?

Listen carefully to the following statement. It's extra. You are not paying for it.

The statement is: There is more to life than sex.

Yes, you've heard that phrase before. It is not especially deep or revealing. This is not to take away from that reality that sex is a most pleasurable and spiritual experience. But ask yourself:

Are you willing to put up with XYZ just to be able to mee between the sheets?

Is how good he is in bed your most importan consideration?

What traits or flaws are you willing to over look?

No one is perfect. Oh, you believe you are? Well, we will explore that issue in a future chapter.

Back to your potential partner.

▲ Can you live with his flaws?

If you find your mystical imagery of a prince, will you attempt to shape him to fit your expectations?

Are you still expecting your kiss to turn a frog into a prince?

Dr. Laura Schlessinger, family therapist and author of *10 Stupid Things Women Do To Mess Up Their Lives* wrote, "If you kiss a toad, you get acid in your mouth."

▲ Was he a frog when you met him?

Do you believe things that irritate you now will get better with time?

Are you just settling?

A philosophy that would guide my personal selection process was first introduced in the previously mentioned book, *Love, Loving & Being Loved*. The theory presented was developed after encountering a quantity of men but not experiencing the standard of quality expected. It was at this point that I felt the need to develop an intelligent process for the elimination of non-compatible individuals. Ironically, the question frequently asked of me from men desiring the development of a relationship, is the question, "What do you look for in a person?" Their objective, to establish that they met the requirements (whatever they were), led to the development of the "SESPF" system. Do not try to pronounce it. It has no sound but it represents what I have determined to be the essential qualities necessary for me in a mate.

This is my "**personal**" criterion and response to the many books, articles and talk shows that attempt to influence my selection process. There are those that, after hearing my qualification, have expressed that my standards are too high. My response to them? If you plan to spend the rest of your life with a person, is it not essential to make an informed, carefully thought out choice?

In a local newspaper, an astrological forecast suggested that I would be entering a new 13-year cycle on the 10th (of that month). It stated this would emphasize a deeper intensity of my feelings, along with a desire for more significant relationships. The article continued indicating the first sign of this trend might appear in a new or ongoing twosome. Nothing here sounds unusual. The point? It went on to suggest that **LOWERING** my expectations a little will maintain harmony between the mystery man and me.

No, I am not having a senior moment. Are you curious or wonder what the "SESPF" system represents? Let me explain. The characteristics that are of paramount importance to my ideal are listed in the "must have's" below. The essential factors are in rank order of importance:

Spiritual
Emotional
Social
Physical
Financial

The *Spiritual* represents the man who is spiritually connected. I did not say a religious man. Religion does not equal spirituality. For me, it is the man who has placed God at the head of his life. To be spiritually directed does not mean the person must run for the church doors every time they open. It does mean that he maintains an intimate, daily relationship with God, being

71

able to hear from him. Where is his heart? Does he have a heart after God? My father, Pastor Lawrence W. Boone, once said to me, "How can you expect a man to faithful to you if he is not first faithful to God?"

The impact of that statement hit me like a whack upside the head, when I came to understand it's deep revelation and implications. A track by the Tract League, Grand Rapids, Michigan, lists the ideal man as the man who puts God's business above his own affairs. He teaches and sets a good example for his family and reads the Word of God with as much diligence as he does the daily paper. For many, being with a person on a spiritual, emotional level is not a value. For me, the spiritual supersedes the other desired characteristics. It is number **ONE**. This area is the core of a relationship. Though a couple comes together through the sex act (the closest they can be physically) they remain separate entities.   Only through the spirit can they become singularly connected. The search for the "Soul mate" becomes the ultimate goal because of the desire for that close connectedness. It is the desire to be understood. What the man and woman needs to understand is if they seek to develop and grow closer to each other, there is a better way. The following illustration demonstrates that as they each grow towards God, they become closer to each other.

GOD

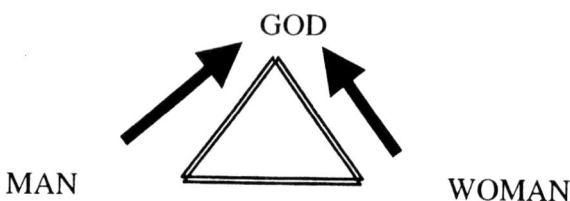

MAN   WOMAN

Paulette Pearson, the wife of Denzele Washington, when asked the question, "How do you handle the fame?" responded, "Without a spiritual base we couldn't deal with it." Their success is no mystery to me.

The next category is the *Emotional* that represents emotional stability. Is he sane or emotionally stable? I do not think that is too much to ask, do you? At the prompting of a friend, I looked up the word "sane." The definition included: rational, logical, sound, sober, sensible, normal. The word "normal" may be questionable. Who of us is "normal?" My own conclusions involved questions that led to the development of my definition of "sane." Is he supportive and understanding? Or is he carrying excess baggage from his childhood or a past relationship that will interfere with your present relationship? We all do but to what degree? Is he prepared to let go, move forward into the present and the future? How you are treated by the male in your life is related to his excess baggage. It is related to his experiences with women from his past. Does he have the ability to laugh or is his daily language pattern negative? Is he emotionally shallow and uninvolved?

In a relationship, putting up with a partner that remains emotionally distant and provides little emotional support places a tremendous strain on the relationship. It is equally important that a relationship be emotionally satisfying.

The *Socially Adaptable* man is a man who is as comfortable in a formal setting (when dressed in a tuxedo) as he is when dressed casually and placed in an informal setting. With this man, you are relaxed in any setting because you are not afraid of his being unmannerable (picking his nose or belching uncontrollably or worst). He utilizes his great sense of humor. You can introduce him to family and friends and not be fearful of what he might say. After all, he is a reflection of your good judgment. Being well read, he can converse on a variety of subjects. Sounds like fun? He is.

The importance of the *Physical*? Not really. I am not interested in a relationship based on the physical. Subconsciously, the physical plays an equal part. Everyone has a set of physical requirements. It is not unimportant or insignificant. If it was not a factor it would not be included in the five "must have's." Growing up I heard the phrase, "Do not judge a book by it's cover." Yet I can recall on occasion, entering the library, unsure of what I wanted and what did I do? Probably the same thing you did. I looked at the cover and read the jacket before taking out the book.

Now I ask you, how much weight does physical attractiveness carry?

Society, the media, places a great deal of value on the physical. The media has begun advertising the physical attributes of men in commercials. The commercials include Calvin Klein, Bugle Boy, Coke, etc. Movies now subject men to the same exploitation previously experienced by women. The stereotypical presentation promotes the ideal man as: scantily clothed, buffed, physically fit, with chiseled features, creating a totally powerful, sexual look. But to whom? Is it still true that beauty is in the eye of the beholder? How much of this do we buy into? What is beauty or a totally gorgeous look?

Bishop T.D. Jakes recently stated in an audiotape: "Machoism may get her but it won't keep her. Superman has gone out of style. It's Clark Kent that everybody's looking for now."

The partner selected does not have to be attractive in the reflection of anyone else's eyes, but your own. You have heard the phrase, "Beauty's only skin deep but ugly is to the bone?" Well, maybe you have not heard it quite that way. The statement can also be true for a person who has a knock down, drop dead dazzling exterior (according to society) but be "ugly" to the bone. A man can be strong and physically attractive and weak emotionally. What is inside will show itself and reflect in the outer appearance. In the July issue of Ebony Men magazine, the writer of an article stated, "The physical part is secondary. What's most important is a one-to-one connection."

The soul is always dealing with the essence of things. Not the form. Do not mistake lust for the physical with true love. The physical appearance may get your attention but it is not a good reason to become emotionally involved or emotionally invested.

The *Financial* factor represents financial stability. It refers to the individual that has his finances in balance. It does not mean he has to be wealthy or debt free. It does mean he is financially responsible. The man that views money as a tool to be utilized to enhance and enjoy life is a man in balance.

This trait is listed last in rank order indicating that it is not the most important factor. However, financial resources are essential and, as previously mentioned, prove to be a source of friction within a relationship. The ability to be able to make a spontaneous decision to travel or visit the theater, should only be limited by your time schedule.

The "SESPF" system shared was developed to enable a person to recognize when they are receiving less than their established standard. At times it is hard to identify but you can sense when things are not right. The majority will not fulfill the requirements of your discriminating taste. They will not qualify and prove to be incompatible.

Characteristics you feel to be essential may be missing from my list. During a television broadcast, John Gray, author of *Men are From Mars and Women are From Venus*, expounded on what women and men look for. His list included:

For women:

Affection
Honesty
Openness
Financial Support
Family Commitment
And to feel prized and cherished at all times

For men:

Sexual fulfillment
Recreational companion
Attractive spouse
Domestic Support

And Admiration

The standard by which one operates is an individual choice. You may list other particulars or desires that are "must have's." For some, a well-educated man is a priority while someone else seeks someone who is street smart. The significance is not in my preference for you or yours for me. The image of which you are attracted to is largely determined in childhood and recorded in your memory. It is only that you establish your own guidelines. The characteristics you seek will not be equally present in each relationship or exhibited equally all the time. But they are present. An illustration from Laughter, the Best Medicine (Readers Digest) tells of a woman speaking to her friend about her two beaus, "If I could combine their qualities, I'd be the happiest person in the world. Ronald is rich, handsome and witty. Tony wants to marry me."

Jean Kerr once said, "Marrying a man is like buying something you've been admiring for a long time in a shop window. You may love it when you get it home but it doesn't always go with everything."

Hold on. Before you agree. The statement does not mean you should ask for a refund. Sometimes the traits that originally attracted you to the person, become character flaws that eventually cause you to withdraw. For example, someone with the trait of being spontaneous and exciting is later viewed as undependable and unpredictable. A man's ability to take charge and make decisions may initially be acknowledged and attractive. However, his take charge spirit may become annoying with time when your input is not requested nor appreciated. Later you grow to see your partner as domineering and controlling. Remember the old adage, "Be careful what you ask for. You just may get it."

In her book, *If I'm So Wonderful, Why Am I Still Single,* author Susan Page presents an exercise that asks singles to think about their partner and their relationship. They are asked to list everything they would change about their partner if they had a magic wand. The items are then labeled N=Nuisance and EF=essential flaw.

Again the question:

Can you live with your conclusions? Even if someone looks like the Prince Charming of your dreams, you might be completely turned off once engaged in conversation. Some things are worth whatever you have to go through but are you willing?

If after your evaluation you discover many character defects, are you willing to lower your standards?

▲ How can you stay with a man that does not share your fundamental beliefs? Having things in common include basic values. What is important to you and the relationship?

Are you settling for a second class relationship?

Why settle for a substandard product?

Are you settling for less and hoping for more?

You will find you will end up like the McDonald's slogan with change back from a dollar. If you do not expect much, you do not get much. The price you put on your head is the price people will pay.

Maybe for you the opposite is true. I hope it is though I have encountered more women in the previous camp. Perhaps the high standard with which you carry yourself becomes the focus of well meaning friends. Friends that suggest that you will be alone all of your life because your standards are too high. Possibly a horoscope may even suggest you lower your standards.

Here is where the paradigm continues.

If you lower your standard, will you be happy or satisfied with what you attract? Will you be a better person because of the relationship?

If your answer is no, then take courage. Do not compromise or fake interest rather than face the aloneness. If you fear the lack of intimacy, emptiness will become a constant companion. Ask yourself, can I live with this person for the rest of my life? Marriage was designed to be for a lifetime, though the words of commitment "until death do us part" have been eliminated from most ceremonies. It has become "until love do us part." This is a sad commentary on the status of marriage and the level of commitment. Someone may say, "Well, if it is till death do us part, somebody is about to die." Wait a minute.

For those of you that are too emotionally exhausted to do anything about it and go on more out of habit than desire, there is hope. The solution is not in creating superficial relationships but in knowing yourself and

ACCEPTING MEN FOR WHO THEY ARE:
Prince or Frog?

Is your immediate reaction, "What do you mean FROGS?" Have you forgotten the Once-Upon-A-TIME fairy tale with which this book began? The story created the MENtal imagery of Frogs as symbolic of men. Why?

Remember your last experiences with FROGS? Was it in high school in your biology class? Does that flash back produce warm, pleasant thoughts? Were you particularly interested in the anatomy of the frog when the instructor presented it? When requested, along with the group, to handle, dissect and label the frog, did you embrace the assignment with enthusiasm? Or was it a necessary evil needed for a grade? For some maybe it was enjoyable. For most it was not. Yuck. Why the disdain?

Unlike little boys, with exceptions, little girls did not grow up capturing and playing with frogs as pets. Boys were described in rhymes as "Nails, snails and puppy dog tails" and frogs. In fairy tales, frogs symbolized the negative, unattractive victim who was always seeking assistance from a pretty young thing. Sound familiar?

In most societies the socialization process is innately designed to keep the sexes separated until the pre-teen era, longer if possible. During adolescence, the phase noted for the most dramatic changes, the genders take a new interest in each other. Not only are they learning to communicate but their hormones are doing a serious number on their emotions.

The female begins to wonder about this strange species, wanting to understand their anatomy. She begins to desire to explore what she has been told "not to touch." While window shopping in Chicago, I noticed a T-shirt in the window. It was a cartoon caricature of a little nude boy and girl. They are drawn so their backs are to you. The little girl looks at the little boy and asks, "Can I touch it?" He replies, "No, yours already fell off." The cartoon illustrates the mystic and the false notions of the genders.

The female wonders just who are they, the male gender? At just about the same time, the male is attempting to come to terms with the same questions about himself.

. On the tombs and pyramids found in the land known as Kemit (Egypt) is a spiritual warning. "Man Know Thy Self." For most, the phrase means to know what significant people in your environment think of you. In this usage, the term "Man" applies to all of mankind. Identity is the end result of how others perceive and respond to you. The phrase, "Know Thy Self" is a warning to be careful. Who you believe you are is a result of who you think you are not. The literal package is put together by others.

Thus the complexity of the challenge.

Where and how does a male learn to become "a man?" From the streets? His peers? His father?

Tim La Hay, an author and speaker, writes, "It is harder to be a man today than it was in your father's or grandfather's time, for conditions and customs have changed."

Since 1970, the increase in single parent households has left the majority males living in female headed households.

References in the book entitled, *The Male Temperament*, Tim LaHay pointed to "the liberal policies of current humanistic thought....and an educationally bankrupt public school system as one of the reasons for an increase in modern cop outs."

That is not new information. In fact, the book was copy written in 1977. It is written in scripture, "There is nothing new under the sun." (Ecclesiastics 1:9).

The socialization of the male child includes the educational system. The male child attends a head start program and then elementary school where, it is reported, approximately 83-99% of the teachers are female. Attend an elementary school program if you have further doubts of the validity of the statement.

Considering the statistical information, the critical question becomes, how can a female teach a male to be a "man?"

The socialized conditioning process continues with influence from another arena:

Religion

Visit a religious service, except for the Muslim faith (there may be others), and you will find a female majority in attendance. From the positions of Sunday school teacher to clergy, the male child observes female leadership in action. Again the question, how does he learn? Where are the strong male role models to teach? In the book, *Fire In The Belly*, author John Bly wrote, "men aren't taught to be men."

Without individuals, males, who are willing to be teachers, the youth responds to the media's images. What imagery does the media project? Often that of George Jefferson, Al Bundy and Bill Cosby. Even in cartoons the caricatures are portrayed as weak, henpecked buffoons. A small sample representation includes: George Jetson, Dagwood Bumstead, Fred Flintstone and Homer Simpson.

Do your own analysis. Without strong males to emulate and images of fathers that hug, who will set the pattern? The mothers. So one may ask, "Then are the women at fault?"

The situation brings to mind a conversation overheard between two old friends. The story relates the return of a man to his old neighborhood. Having obtained success in his field, he began looking around the neighborhood with disdain. After observing the amount of crime, drugs and debris in the area, he turned to his friend, a resident. "Why is the neighborhood so bad?" he asked. His friend's answer was short and curt, "You left." Fathers have relinquished their responsibilities to the mothers. For any number of reasons, they have gone AWOL (absent without leave) and the women have had to step up to the plate. Not a desired position but a necessary one for the survival of their families.

During a workshop with a group of veterans, a male made the following statement, in response to the above question. "You are right. My mother raised me and taught me how to be a man. I think she did a darn good job." To which I replied, "Yes, your mother raised you right (accepting his definition of right), but how can a female teach you the aspects of what it is to be a male? It is true that sons are greatly influenced by their mothers. They learn how to relate to women and the general populous, but to be a man? How can I teach what I have not experienced? It is much like a person who blindfolds him or herself because they want to experience what it is like to be blind. That person will never know how it feels to be blind because they can return, at any moment, to being a sighted person. They can empathize but not feel the real.

Society places pressure on the male to achieve, yet does not provide him with the tools necessary to succeed. Men are encouraged to earn an income to provide a living for his family but not taught to display the deep emotions of living.

An excerpt from an article written by playwright and performance poet, Carl Hancock, illustrates the plight. Though the author alludes to the difficulties of the African-American man, the problem of emotional distance appears to be cross-cultural.

He writes, "This kind of expression was not typical in my upbringing. Intimacy seemed synonymous with sex to me. I had never hugged (or been hugged) by my father, held hands or kissed the face of my brothers. Maintaining casual eye contact with other men was uncomfortable. I thought intimacy, when it could be achieved was something men reserved for women, our mothers, girlfriends and wives."

Carl Hancock is a playwright and performance poet who, at the writing of the article, resided in Brooklyn.

The objective of this chapter is to define "a man," and to assist the female gender in the development of a greater understanding of men.

But WAIT. I am sure you can tell by my name that I am a woman. Yet here I am attempting to define "a man." Is that not just like a woman? So, I acknowledge that what I present here is my perceptions of the realities of "being a man" along with various authors.

In the *Coming Of Age*, by Paul Hill, Jr., defines manhood in America as being closely tied to the acquisition of wealth; health is a power to control others. Understand, again, this is the box America has placed the man and the woman in.

My experience in raising two male children, Eric now 25 years of age and Raffael age 21 (at the time of this writing), has taught me a necessary survival technique. As a single parent for the majority of their years, it was necessary for the survival of my sons to surround them with men. Men who had a strong definition of themselves and were willing to share themselves with them. "Any woman worth her salt knows how important it is to get her boys to become men."

These words by Dr. T. Garrott Benjamin emphasize the challenge (of mothers) to cut the apron strings.

So what is the answer?

You still have not succinctly defined "a man." How can we accept them for who they are if we do not know who they are? "We can only love what we know." First consider, that there are no simple answers to complex problems. So the explanation will begin with what men are not:

They are not:

PERFECT

They are not:

Your Knight In Shining Armour, Come To Rescue You
And Take You To Happy Land

Charles Swindoll in his book, ***The Grace Awakening***, said, "Every bride who thinks she's married a knight in shining armour had better stock up on polish, because the tarnish sets in quickly."

They are not:

Superhuman
Or
Saintly

Here's a side note to the men that may be reading this book: You can now exhale. Take a deep breath, release the pressure and exhale. Relax and be who you are.

What a man does is a result of who he is. It is the wise woman who understands that men are **human.**

Lorraine Hansberry's award-winning play, *Raisin In The Sun,* produced the following advice: "It's when he's at his lowest and can't believe in himself cause the world done whipped him so. When you start measuring somebody, measure him right child, measure him right. Make sure you done taken into account what hills and valleys he come through before he got to where he is."

Men struggle to establish their own identity as males. Every man is different. They are a product of their environment. Their training, education and life experience make-up the sum total of who they are. Men are taught by cultural cues that to express emotions openly make you less of a man. What is acceptable and unacceptable has been established by someone else, early in their lives. Their reaction to you is a result of their previous experience with women.

An example from my life came from my son, Eric. Early in his young adult life, I watched Eric's reaction to the females in his life at the time. I then asked the question of him, "Why are you so hard when relating to the female?" His answer reflected the sentiments of many. "Mom, when I treat them with kindness and I am nice to them, they dog me. They take my kindness for weakness. When I act like I don't care, they are all over me." The statement created a new level of understanding for me. My son's reaction to the next female that entered his life, would not initially be based on anything having to do with her. Except that she is a female. His struggle to develop and establish how he will operate in his manhood will be the result of time-tested experiences, good or bad.

Men are in pain that is deeper than the exterior has the ability to express. They have encountered depreciating conditions, maybe not from you, but often from the one they love. The one

84

that was designed to be their support. You enter the picture, full of expectations based only on a superficial knowledge of who you think they are. Just as your preconceived ideas in the lab told you, before touching it, that the frog would feel slimy. In actuality, the skin is dry and smooth. If you never touched it would never know the truth.

The continued development of a relationship will require that you understand that often men do not have the capacity to give you what you need. It is because they have not experienced it themselves. The only way you can come to know who he is, is to develop your ability to apply patience, to listen and allow him to communicate. Frequently the female will say, "But he is not saying anything." What the female in that situation does not understand is that in effect he is communicating a great deal. Someone once said, "By the time women understand what they (men) are saying, they have stopped listening."

In an attempt to obtain information, women often resort to asking the male, "What are you thinking about?" The response, "Nothing." She then interprets his answer as, he really is stupid or he does not want to communicate. Both patterns of thought can be erroneous. Listening involves hearing what is not being said. Careful study of his behavior will tell you what he is thinking. Out of frustration you ask, "Why does he have to be like that?" (Grammar acknowledged—question formed the way it has frequently been asked.) You look for the answers to, "Why can't he be like me and say what he is thinking?"

ANSWER: He can not be you. **ACCEPT HIM FOR WHO HE IS.**

Waiting for him to change, to become what is desired, creates unrealistic expectations. Rather than trying to change a person, teach. Teach by your example. If they choose to change, great. If not, nagging, or persistent encouraging, will not work.

An excerpt from a magazine (cannot locate the source) describes a conversation that contains a bit of advice: "My friend Ellen says that the way to change a man is to perceive him differently. She perceives her boyfriend, Stan, as an enlightened man eager for an equal partnership, even though in certain areas he's still a flawed man who is striving for the best deal."

Women tend to focus on the weaknesses of the man versus emphasizing his strengths. Therapist Marilyn Graman, who leads a workshop called, Having What You Want In a Man, astutely states, "When we're not attracted to someone, we quickly see his negative qualities. The more attracted we are, the fewer negatives we see." The myth is that with a little prodding he will become whom we expect him to be.

Men are barraged with comparisons and comments that reflect the sentiments that say, "I wish you were more like him. He does this for her and that for her....." Considering conversations with men, the previous verbal style does not have positive results. Men tend to respond with a lackadaisical who cares or "She needs to go get him if she is not satisfied with me." Maybe she (the female that is having things done for her) knows how to treat her man and my partner does not." Making comparisons may force temporal change. Eventually it will create distance. **Accept him for who he is.**

In the words of Henri Frederic Amiel, "It is not what he has, nor even what he does, which directly expresses the worth of a man, but what he is. "Character is what you are in the dark" stated the great theologian D.L. Moody. In the *National Enquirer*, it was said by Merry Browne that one should, "Expect people to be better than they are; it helps them to become better. But don't be disappointed when they are not; it helps them to keep trying."

Listen to the words of Tim LaHay, from his book, *Understanding the Male Temperament*, "You are the only person in the world who can help your husband feel comfortable in his manhood. Work at it---you'll both be richer for it."

> "Things and people are not what we wish them to be or what they seem to be. They are what they are."

(God's Little Instruction Book On Love).

As motivational speaker, Zig Ziglar so aptly put it, "There are no right or wrong characteristics, no good or bad characteristics. We are where we are because of what has gone into our minds. We change where we are and what we are by changing what goes into our minds."

If you are looking for the perfect man versus the real, take note. The perfect does not exist. The judgments as to whether someone is good or bad, is based on your own personal preferences. You are simply readjusting your prejudices."

If you find that you cannot accept him as he is, then of course go *In search of a good man.* Undoubtedly, you will find what you are looking for and then *change* him to be what you wanted.   And it will begin again....Until you learn "finally to appreciate, the people who "happen to be there." Made for us? Thank God, no. They are made for themselves, odder than you could have believed and worth far more than we guessed."   --An excerpt from *The Four Loves* (Harcourt Brace Jovanavich).

Phillip Cole, an associate and friend, reflecting on the allegorical story of the princess and the frog and what it illustrates had this to say: "The fairy tale illustrates that good things   are often found in unattractive packages. The frog never turns out to be a jerk."

Many leave home searching for something. They need only to return home and dig deeper, they would find what they seek, in their own backyard. Motivational speaker Zig Ziglar wrote, "a person will generally get from others precisely what they expect and will always find what they are looking for." Look for the good.

If you who are *In search of a good man* look around yourself. Look for the man who is comfortable with himself. Then accept him for who he is, warts and all.

In search of a good man:

The Dating Game

Has it ever happened that you went out on a date, thought you had a good time, and he never called you back? Or has it been awhile since you played the dating game? Are you unsure of what works or how the game is played? All you have to do is walk by the newsstands. You will be barrage with cover stories in popular magazines that feature a large quantity of advice on the subject of dating and sex. Articles that promise to:

> Make you attractive to the opposite sex
> Give you the secrets to get and keep any man
> Show you seven ways to spot a man you can not trust
> Teach you the How To's of dating
>   And
>
> Help you meet the man of your dreams in 30 days or less

This chapter will include similar information so, as not to disappoint the person looking for answers they have not found on the newsstands. If you are looking for the specifics of where to meet men, what jobs or cities are prominent for meeting men, sorry.

There are articles that will suggest that you go to certain cities (one even suggested Anchorage, Alaska). If information of this specific nature was included, it may be out of date by the printing of this book. Others suggest the dry cleaners (you will know he has clean clothes) or book stores (you will know he can read). My experience has shown me that wherever you are, when you are ready, he will come. Yet a woman responding out of desperation (the wrong motivation) resolves to do the dating scene. The desperation of those seeking is evidenced through the success of the 1-900 numbers. The incredible display of personal want ads in the local newspaper documents the scores of people searching for a mate.

What information has contributed to the increased urgency of women, in particular? A major contributing source has been studies, including research completed at Harvard and Yale Universities in 1994. The study suggested and statistically supported the idea of a man shortage. Later Census bureau reports disputed the findings, predicting that 32% (not 5%) of never married, 35-year old, college educated women would marry by age 65. Men, excited at the prospects of capitalizing on the man shortage theory, began to circulate the data. Phrases frequently heard were similar to: "There's only one man to every 3 or 4 women, baby, you got to share me, I'm your last chance."

So in desperation, the female frequents the club scenes, going out night after night, advertising her availability. She kisses her share of frogs, passes out business cards to whoever feigns an interest and waits for a date.

Can you relate to the above script? Then the following will feel all too real.

Let's say that by sheer statistics (passed out enough business cards) or call it luck of the draw, someone calls and the date is set. The time arrives and you want everything to be right. As he arrives, you check and re-check everything. You glance in the mirror on your way to the door and notice you need to spritz that one hair back in place. After doing a final check for lipstick on the teeth, you answer with a forced smile. It is not forced because you do not want to be there. You recognize the uncomfortability factors are at an all time high. You feel your body heat deodorant being activated as you speak. Your thinking is clouded as you struggle with the greeting. Your thinking pattern leads you to wonder: Will he like me and if he does, will he call again? The difficulties of letting go of past experiences and just enjoying the moment crowd your thinking.

The date continues in quiet, out of the way place. Jerry Seinfeld calls a date "an all night job interview." Your previously selected questions quickly reveal the level of conversation intimidates him. To you, the conversation is boring, your laughter is scripted and the psychological distance increases over the course of the date. The only real accomplishment for the night was that you both seem to agree to disagree. You think "what a waste of a good evening. I should have tried a dating service.

What went wrong? Why do I subject my self to such abuse? Who am I kidding? I want to find a man and dating is an intricate part of the process.

Dating involves a certain amount of risk. Are you really ready to play the dating game? Well, the rules may have changed since you last played the game. Listen up! If you are determined to do this, let's devote some time to a few practical tips.

Your success on the dating scene will be largely dependent on your **ability to communicate**. You can and must learn the art of conversation.

An issue of the Reader's Digest contained a statement by Benjamin Disreal in *Points to Ponder*. "The art of conversation consists of the exercise of two fine qualities: You must originate and you must sympathize; you must possess at the same time the habit of communicating and the habit of listening. The union is rare, but irresistible."

If you have difficulty generating conversation, the solution is simple. Show a genuine interest in the other person. Allow the person to share who they are. Benjamin Disaeli further stated, "Talk to a man about himself and he will listen for hours."

People love to talk about themselves. This does not mean to mindlessly remain uninvolved as the other person talks. Conversation requires you to actively listen and provide feedback that indicates, "I heard what you said." Otherwise you will hear the other person saying things like, "But I told you that the first time we met. Don't you remember?" To actively listen, you must learn to ask targeted questions and listen for the answers.

Most importantly, **maintain eye contact** during the conversation. It is said that the eyes are the seat of the soul. Before a person reacts outwardly to an emotionally impacting

90

statement, they will usually react with their eyes. Remember the old western movies when the gunslingers were standing face to face, preparing to shoot it out? Visualize the scene for a moment: It is usually two men standing at a distance, with their hands down at their sides. As you revisit the intensity of the moment, take notice. Are they watching the other man's hands or their eyes? It is a sure bet that they are watching the eyes. The eyes will reveal when he is ready to reach for his gun.

The failure of conversation often occurs when you allow yourself to be distracted by your surroundings and you lose eye contact. It is amazing how many attempt to communicate with their mate while sitting in front of a television or in a movie theater. It is almost impossible to maintain an uninterrupted thought pattern with those variables. Find a place to be apart, focus and enjoy the mental stimulation that conversation can provide.

An article on dating suggests you not tell all until he is committed...until he is in love with you. The statement poses the question, if you do not open up and share who you are, who is he in love with? A mirrored image of what you thought he wanted? Should you open up and be real? Should you reveal who you are while dating? Obviously, that is the only way he will come to know the real you. "But what if I reveal who I am and he does not like who I am?" Will time change the outcome? No, who you are is all you've got. If he does not like who you are, tomorrow will not change that. Discard the thinking pattern that has trained you to be something you are not. The tricks that taught you to:

Count to five before you answer whether you are available for a DATE

Or

Not accept a Saturday date if he asks after Wednesday

Or

Not return phone calls

Or

Not be ready when he arrives even though
you have been ready for hours.

Lay aside the blank stares and empty smiles you have
learned to use so you would not appear intelligent. These
techniques are useless mind games. The result of the deception is a
waste of valuable time. Besides, if you change who you are and
the way you act for the man, who has the control? Do not be
deceived. There is a large population of good men that are not
intimidated by successful, intelligent women. Do not limit
yourself.

Learn to relax and enjoy the moment, for just what it is.
A moment in time. Realize that the person you are out with has
entered your life for a reason. It may result in a committed
relationship and it may not. Eternity does not depend on this one
moment. To believe that it does, is to create a tension that makes it
impossible to just relax and enjoy the person you are with. An
excerpt from the article, Breaking The Chain Of Impossible
Relationships, "If you approach every date with the idea that this
has to turn into an all consuming love affair, you lose out in 3
ways:

- First, you become uptight and anxious because so much
  is at stake.

- Second, most of all of your social encounters have to be
  counted as failures when measured against your lofty
  goal.

And

- Third, you miss out on a variety of experiences that,
  besides being experiences that, besides being enjoyable
  in themselves, might be intermediate steps toward
  fulfilling love relationships."

Unfortunately, you may quickly realize that the date is not
going to end in a Love Connection or even a doable friendship.
How do you end it, if you conclude that you are not interested in a

continued relationship? If you find that he is just not your type? Do you tell him? Do you promise to call and never do or use empty phrases like, "Let's do it again sometimes? That sounds all too familiar, doesn't it? How did it feel when it was said to you?

The book by Dr. Joy Browne, *Why They Don't Call When They Say They Will—And Other Mixed Signals*, contributes explanations regarding the male gender and their behavior. As a woman, you know you never liked the pretense. Why continue to repeat the cycle?

The first part of this chapter has concentrated on the development of skills that make for an interesting date. But how do you find a **GOOD** man?

A minister speaking to men at a conference stated, "Everyone is looking for a **GOOD** man. The army wants a good man, the church, even the dope dealer wants a good man. And **EVERY** woman wants a **GOOD** man."

On the basis of the previous statement, consider: How will you know if he is good?

A solution being put to use by countless individuals is a service founded by Private investigator Tim Bartlett. Check-A-Mate detective service provides a medium to investigate people you are dating. Tim stated in a magazine article that 80% of his clients are women running background checks. Another source quotes Ralph Thomas, director of the National Association of Investigative Specialist, "About 85,000 women a year use detectives to check on the dependability of the men they are dating. Investigations can include: the purchase of court house records that record the purchase of properties, information on the man's voting patterns, marriages and tax assessments, to name a few."

A sure sign of the times, wouldn't you say? Another alternative is to rent a husband. A retired sheriff from Texas has established a "lending" service called, Rent-A-Husband. This service is targeted to the woman who does not want someone around full-time. Just every now and then. His reasoning for creating the business appears to very practical. He stated, "Single women can be charged as much as $2,000 less for pricey items like cars when they have their *husband* along." Who would have ever thought that was true? For certain, women have come to realize that statement is frequently all too true. Yet is renting a husband the answer?

You have arrived at your point of desperation, not destination. You have conducted phone interviews and did the dating scene. You have discovered that men (women) are on their best behavior during the dating phase, until the introductory offer expires. Out of desperation, you even placed a personal ad in the newspaper.

Again the question, How can I find a good man? To begin, here are two words of advice: *STOP LOOKING.*

When you make a conscious decision to end the search, you will be in a position to meet, if you choose, the man who is to be your soul mate.

After the shock wears thin you may ask, "What do you mean stop looking? How can I find what I am looking for if I stop looking?"

When you are no longer looking, that is when you will find him. He will find you. This theory is supported in scripture, Proverbs 18:22. It says, "Whose **findeth a wife** findeth a good thing, and obtaineth favor of the Lord."

Men are attracted to the woman that has a quiet confident spirit. A woman who has not become consumed by the chase. Remember the reference to dating being like shopping for clothes? Ever had an occasion where you needed to locate a special outfit for an affair? You began a tiring searching. You try on outfit after outfit and nothing seems to fit. After giving up, one day you walk in a store, looking for something incidental and, you guessed it. There is the perfect outfit.

In a special family issue of *Gospel Today*, May/June, 1996 issue, Pastors Mack and Brenda Timberlake offer this in their

Family Ties column: Since we have been Pastors we have found that the people who have gotten the best mates were the ones who were not looking for one. They were totally sold out to God and said, God I'm just going to love you with all of my heart and God gave them a gift of a mate. Those who got distracted and began to wonder, How will I know if this is the one?"...Found themselves in relationships that did not work out. Trust God to bring that special individual into your life. When it happens you will know it"

So who is to do the searching?

Perhaps you are saying, "I am not a particularly religious person, so I will have to search on my own." The principles of truth work for anyone that applies them. Light does not cease to exist because you choose not to believe in it. Someone said, "Man runs after woman until she decides to turn around and catch him." A familiar toast says, "Here's to Woman—who came after man, and who has been after him ever since."

The male radar can detect simmering desperation in the women they encounter. Men respond to the "Either you or me" ultimatum by running in the other direction. The desperation that suffocates men, that threatens their own survival, drives them away. They view that individual as too needy and begin to feel a sense of a loss of self.

If you sense the pulling away of the man you have taken an interest in, you may be weighing the question: To bed or not to bed. You may decide to trade your convictions in an attempt to hold on to him and to fulfill your own need to be held on to. What you are attempting to achieve is connectness, as previously mentioned. However, to compromise your boundaries does not accomplish what you seek. To become physical, interrupts the development and growth of the relationship. The focus changes and often prohibits moving to the next level. The first physical contact becomes the turning point in the relationship. Whether you go to bed or not is purely subjective. If you choose to go to bed, out of some sense of obligation (he spent a lot of money on the date) or to satisfy your physical needs, it is a lose/lose situation.

When you give your body to another, you are sharing something you can never get back.

Though you may feel there are no strings attached, it is to return to previously mentioned spider web. The strings are apparently invisible yet deadly to the one caught unaware. Struggle as you might to be released, the web becomes a place of discontent and consuming bondage. There are many that will say to you, "Naw girl, I went to bed with a man on the first date and we dated for another, good six months." Evaluate the results.

The choice is ultimately yours. The alternative is to change your focus from outward to inward. It is to work on the development of you. It is to learn to be an interesting person. In my experience, the women that desperately wanted to meet someone remained alone. Those that became interested in life and began to enjoy it, apart from a relationship, were the ones that were surrounded by interested people. People (male and female), who were drawn to the vibrant energy and excitement the person generated. The attraction factor. Smile and make yourself more approachable.

Attraction to others is manifested through:

YOUR MIND AND YOUR PERSONALITY. It is whatever makes you uniquely you.

The author of *Winning the Age Game* says, "A man is intrigued and challenged by a woman who is an interesting person in her own right, whose personality has enough depth to provide that essential ingredient for any successful relationship between men and women—the masculine need for meaningful conquest."

INNER CONFIDENCE

A woman at peace within herself, with who she is, will exude the inner confidence that attracts.

APPEARANCE

The evaluation of your appearance will be based on the quality and good taste exhibited by your choice of attire.

It is summertime and you pull out your favorite open toed sandals. You are conscious of your need to paint your toes but you miss another detail:

Ashy ankles and Heels.

No, uh, uh, do not reach for that jar of Vaseline?

Jar of Vaseline? Yes. Major idioms have been passed down from generation to generation as tips. You know the techniques you were taught to save time or money? They included how to:

* Stop a run in your panty hose with fingernail polish or to place the run on the inside of your leg

* Secure a loose or missing button with a safety pin

* Replace a missing garter fastener with a penny (a little tricky)

This includes good hygiene. This goes without saying yet it is necessary to mention it here. Nothing turns a man off quicker than body odor and/ or bad breath. Think about it: How can he whisper in your ear if he is apprehensive about coming any closer?

Getting a little personal? Great. Let's continue, if you are committed to getting this right.

Here are a few questions to help you take a personal inventory. Take the quiz, as your personal introduction to the next chapter on *I'm All That and A Bag of Chips.*

▲   What about you attract a person to you?

How do you prepare to meet a potential love interest?

What are your strong points?

What are your weaknesses?

Does your initial impression create the positive, confident, allure you seek?

Are you charismatic or do you simply leak attitude?

Do you need an attitude adjustment?

Have you taken inventory to discover what you have to offer?

Just keep in mind that the extra effort you take to become the right person will prepare you to meet the right person. If he is a good man when he meets you, he will be a better man because of having met you.

You will discover the importance of being and enjoying who you are versus looking for Mr. Right. Now that you have turned your energies inward, ask yourself. Am I really all that? Your reply: *"I'M ALL THAT AND A BAG OF CHIPS."* You don't say. Well, let's go deep and find out.

POTATO **CHIPS**
(PACKED WITH POWER...)

"There is nothing noble about being superior to some other man. The true nobility is in being superior to your previous self."

Hindu proverb

CHAPTER 5

I'M ALL THAT AND A BAG OF CHIPS

Mirror, mirror on the wall,

Who's the fairest of them all?

ME.

You have seen it and met them. Women who believe they are all that and a peanut butter and jelly sandwich. Women who operate daily on the "ME first" basis. The "Princess" mentality. In conversation men describe them as never being satisfied and always wanting more. Taking much but giving nothing. Women that feel they have evolved levels above the average male mentality. She applauds the statement by Josh Billing, that "Every man has a perfect right to his opinion, provided it agrees with ours.

Men list, as one of the major turn off's, a woman that talks about herself too much. So how do you answer the question, "Tell me about yourself?" How often do you mention the "I" word during conversation? Is the focus I, Me, We or Thee?

Destroying the "Princess Myth"

Those that aspire to the "Princess" mentality, listen up. Many want to claim the right to live the life style of an elevated status but do not understand the requirements associated with the position. Think about it. Carrying the title means you must be prepared for close scrutiny in public and in private. Your every move is critiqued and criticized. Consider the amount of money that is required simply to maintain the wardrobe of a Princess. Your appearance becomes the topic of the day, especially if you have committed a faux pas. Those that barely know you analyze your life style and feel they have a right to do so based on your status. You give up the freedom to be real, for a public façade, a necessity of the title you wear. Still enchanted with the position? "Yes," you emphatically state, adding, "If I am a princess, that means there are many prince's willing to finance the arrangement because *I Am All That*."

Let's look at the downside, if there is one. What happens when you become pregnant and gain 10, no, 20 pounds? Will those that are in love with the image remain your loyal subjects or will your lover eventually abandon you in search of another? Or it occurs one day that you do not feel like perpetrating by smiling or giving the princess wave to those you interface with on that particular day?

Oh, it is understood that you can get any man that you go after and if you are having a bad day, so be it. Right? Reflect on the numerous lovers of your pass. How long did they stay? Three months? Six? The statement, "I can get any man I want" is frequently said but the question becomes, "Do you have what it takes to keep him?" Or is your response easily, "NEXT."

Benjamin Whichcote describes the results: "None are so empty as those who are full of themselves."

Men are initially fascinated with your Royal Highness. **With time,** your "make me happy, my wish is your command, serve me" mentality soon wears thin. They (men) begin to see the cracks in the mystic as the "real" you inevitably emerge. The burden of trying to always be all that becomes a tiresome, laborious chore. For the male, to assume total responsibility for your happiness is too much for any one person to accept. Along with being responsible for your happiness, the princess mentality says the men are required to know the rules. But wait, if you are constantly changing the rules of the game, shouldn't you let all the players know? Not like the rules listed on a T-shirt that is probably purchased solely by women. A few of the rules listed are:

*   The female always makes the Rules.

* The rules are subject to change at anytime without prior notification.

* No male can possibly know all the rules.

* If the female suspects the Male knows all the rules, she must immediately change some or all the rules.

* The female is never wrong.

If you have the Princess mentality, the above rules are probably part of your belief system. As was previously stated, "Will you ever be satisfied with what any one person has to offer?"

While watching a talk show, my curiosity was aroused when the topic was announced. The topic for the day was, "I will only date men with muscles." Hear me out. The topic does represent the decline in relevancy... yet it was being treated as a serious subject. What caught my attention were the females featured on the show. They boasted of how their rejected admirers reacted to their repulse based on their (the male) anatomy. A few even appeared on the show to provide explanation and justification. While listening to the females reasoning, an astute audience member finally voiced my particular sentiments that said, "You're not all that. What do you bring to the table?" Thank you.

The Princess myth is dead. It is time for real women to stand up and take their place.

Up to this point the focus of, *If I'm Looking For A Prince, Why Am I Kissing Frogs*, has been men and relationships with them. The focus will now shift to the core of it all. YOU. Though you are the foundation, the text of the book could not begin here. If it had, it would have lost the majority of the target population. WOMEN. Perhaps by the time you arrive at this chapter, I have gained your trust. At least enough of your trust to hear me out and weigh the data.

Let's look at the bottom line:

What shape are you in?

Though clothing will cover a multitude of sins, what do you see when you stand naked before a full-length mirror? It is understood that you must love your body the way it is. Yet are there areas for improvement? Do you trust your own evaluation? If not, ask a friend. No, not while you are naked. Ask when you put on those spandex pants or daisy dukes and prepare to go out into the community at large (pun intended).

▲ If you require a man to have money, do you have money?
Do you possess the social graces and emotional stability you seek in the opposite gender?
What message does your image project about you?
Are you broadcasting the wrong message?

Rate your own behavior in a previous relationship. You may discover you need work. It is only after an objective introspection and evaluation (of your own feelings), can you take a look at why men behave the way that they do. "What you dislike in another take care to correct in yourself." Thomas Sprat

Young women have claimed the right to use explicitly, sexually oriented, vulgar language. It appears as if the environment or situation they are in has no influence on how they conduct themselves. In my day, it was unheard of to witness a female, (though it may have been her custom in private), speaking in a loud, provocative manner in public. Anthropologist Margaret Mead voiced the concern that the behavior of women has liberated the men, more than women. She wrote, "For now that women use these terms, men no longer need to watch their own language in the presence of women."

The way you carry yourself will speak louder than any words. If you adopt a style that is loud and vulgar, expect a similar response from those you encounter. Take a personal inventory. List your positive and negative characteristics.

You say you cannot see them? Then *you better ask somebody (state with attitude).* Ask your family, your associates and your friends. After a thorough examination, step back and evaluate the results: How can you seek to attract what you do not already posses? Though it is often said that opposites attract, the familiar practice is to spend time with people who are like us. Let's be real. How often do you go to lunch or dinner with someone you hate? It's not very likely. Johann Wolgang von Goethe said, "Know thyself? If I knew myself, I'd run away."

Pindar wrote, "Learn what you are and be such." Is not that part of the problem? Human beings are caught up in the business of what they are (the social labeling) versus seeking to understand who they are. Pastor Lawrence Boone calls them, human doings instead of human beings. But how can I be who I am if I do not know who I am? How can I come to know the **WHOLE ME?** How can I know what I am seeking if it is a mystery to me?

These are Good questions that deserve an answer. The answer comes in learning how to *FILL THE HOLE IN THE SOUL WITH THE WHOLE essence OF YOU.*

A HOLE IN THE SOUL?

Fill it with the whole you.

A television advertisement for chicken features a woman sitting on the beach. As she speaks, her words demonstrate her lament. She repeats, her voice filled with passion, the words, "Emptiness, Emptiness. How can I fill this emptiness?" Out from behind the rocks, a man appears, dressed in business attire. With an air of authority and matter-of-fact attitude, he responds as if the solution is simple. He answers, "That's easy. EAT something."

In his book, *Love Hunger*, Dr. James Dobson, established that often a person will eat in an attempt to fill, what appears to be a natural hunger. In reality, the surface need for physical food is the result of a deeper desire. Through additional insights the individual discovers it is a love hunger they are trying to satisfy. In effect, it is to try to fill the hole in the soul with that which cannot be physically satisfied. Within my immediate environment, I regularly encounter 14 and 15 year old girls (age not exclusive) who believe they want a baby. They are little girls that should be playing with boys and toys but end up with bottles and babies and wonder WHY? In truth, they want is a baby to hold to feel loved themselves. It is their attempt to fill the hole in the soul with physical touch. What they do not realize is that what they really want is to replace the love they did not receive as a child. They believe they know what love is because of adults who have misrepresented love through: the family system, pornography, media images etc. The adults then point the finger and place the blame on the irresponsibility of the youth, which is acting on their perceived knowledge of truth.

The words of a songwriter described their search as, "Looking for love in empty bottles and cans, looking for love in a woman or a man."
And I add ...or a baby.

During the writing of the above text an insight occurred which required a change in the wording. The original text read, "who believe they want a child." It was then I recognized the need to change the word. A child represents responsibility.

No, they want a baby and are unaware of the enormous amount of endurance required to raise a child.

What is the hunger and how did it come to be? They hunger and long for someone to give them unconditional love. There are many authors with books on the market that provide lengthy explanations on the development of the hunger theory. In essence, they are striving to supplement their diet.

The objective of this chapter is to present a formula for finding the essence of "the Lost Self" Only you can fill the "Hole" in your soul with a "Whole" you. The "real" you. The "you" that is ever present like a small, still running, underground stream. The stream that flows freely underground, waiting for the opportunity, that will allow it to spring forth. The best qualities you possess reside deep inside.

In Search of YOU: The Formula

Picture yourself at a social event.

Before arriving, you determine that you are single and ready to mingle. In an attempt to get to know you, the questioning begins. How do you respond to the question, "Who Are You?"

The first most natural response is to answer by providing your name. Additional information may include that you are a parent, wife, student, employee, and etceteras. Yet, the above responses do not answer the question, "Who are you?" The descriptors utilized are not the sum and substance of who you are.

Let's examine your answers further.

Your name... is not who you are. Your parents gave your name to you, even before they had any knowledge of your personality or who you would become. If your name IS who you are, who do you become if you change your name? Actors regularly use a stage name.

The additional information you provided does not define who you are. Being a mother, wife, member of the First Church motherboard, student or employee not who you are. These titles are roles you fulfill on a daily basis, that may or may not add significance to your life. But let's say for the sake of argument, you say, "I **am** a mother. My life **is** wrapped up in my children. Their schedule **is** my schedule."

▲ What happens when your children grow away and leave for college or marriage? The Empty-nest syndrome? What now? What happens when you are no longer active in those roles? If your life has been on hold, how do you cope?

There are couples that report have had to begin again learning each other after the children moved on. They discovered their day-to-day conversations, with each other, had surrounded issues of the children.

As previously mentioned, your explanation of who you are, may include "wife". If who you are is packaged in being a wife to someone, what happens when your mate says, "I'm leaving on the Midnight Train to Georgia?" When the relationship comes to an end, do you cease to exist?

If you are willing to look deeper, ask yourself:
Is who I am defined by my physical appearance?
What societal messages have defined the development of my outside package? What media messages have I accepted?

Pay close attention to the commercials you hear on a regular basis while watching your favorite television program. Commercials tell you if you do not like who you are you can change it. Don't like your hair color? There is Ms. Clairol. Don't like your breast size, take a trip to Silicon Valley. Women have been sold on the idea of breast implants to enhance their figure. The first woman to pioneer the idea was in 1966. Models believe in, to compete with other models, the virtues of breast enlargement. Too expensive? Now there's the Miracle bra that will push it up and out, creating the illusion of more. Eye color a problem? Within one-hour you can walk out of your optician's office with blue, hazel or green eyes. Whatever your pleasure; It's only a thought and a few dollars away. Just when you think you've got it all together, the media says, "Now let's talk about your breath, your underarm, feet, and so on and so on. Does any message say, "You're okay just like you are?" No, that would not sell products.

A most disconcerting display of the impact of the messages received was exhibited on a television talk show. The guest on the talk show was a 12-year-old girl, accompanied by her mother that wanted a nose job. The request was not a result of a disfiguring accident. It would be cosmetic surgery to improve her appearance. The mother was in total support of her daughter's desire. The questions that surfaced, for me, were not asked during the taping of that show. No discerning audience member or talk show host asked the following:

Had anyone explored with the child what subconscious messages she was acting on? Whose responsibility is to develop her inner self?

Women grow up believing the messages that promote the idea that to value self, you must do more. The "do more mentality" can include losing weight, earning more or having a child. To the individual, she always appears to be competing with someone thinner, younger, prettier or brighter. Indeed, she is unaware that she is competing with their image and more importantly, with her own subconscious view of herself. Dr. Maxwell Maulx, plastic surgeon and author of Psycho Cybernetics stated, "The most important discovery is the self-image."

It was reported that Dr. Maulx was once requested by a client to fix her nose. To the plastic surgeon, the woman's nose appeared to be already perfect. Unable to convince her, the surgery was performed. After completion of the surgery, he asked the client, "How do you like it? to which she replied, "I still feel ugly."

Did you notice the key word? FEEL? Though the nose was a distraction to her, it was not the major contributor to how she perceived herself. "The problem was not the outer skin but the inner man." Percy Sutton

Another example is provided in the fairy tale of Cinderella and Her Three Wicked stepsisters. Cinderella lived with her three stepsisters, whom she thought were all that. Her perception was that she could not compete. Cinderella's low self-esteem caused her to **see herself** in a subservient role. In the book, *A Woman's Worth,* author Marianne Williamson, so aptly confirmed that, "At every moment, a woman makes a choice between the state of the queen and the state of the slave girl. In our natural state, we are glorious beings."

Cinderella accepted the role of a servant as her natural state in life, much like many women in the real world. It is the set image you have of yourself, of who you are in every area of life, which governs your behavior. The mental picture you hold will either aid in your growth or stunt it.

Author Lucius Lewis, in his book *A Better Way of Taking Care Of You* talks about your responsibility. He affirms that "Ultimately, you must decided what you will allow to govern your life...Your willingness to decide to move forward is very necessary to your improvement in personal growth."

Self-love can only come from the inside out. A sense of self-worth can only come from inner acceptance. To accept that you may never wear a size 10 again or that you will never be Mrs. Suzy homemaker. However, the usual occurrence is to continually seek validation from husband, peers, children, employer or anyone within a 1-mile radius. It reminds me of entering a parking lot and receiving a parking receipt. Upon entering the place business (your destination), the receptionist says, "Do you need validation?" To which you respond readily and immediately, "Yes." You eagerly embrace the privilege of validation, which frees you from the responsibility of paying. Validation from an external source frees the individual from internal responsibility.

Consider:

If you are not for you, who will be?
If you are only for you, what's the purpose?

If not now, when?

Hillel

Imagine the following scene:
You attend a social event and you notice someone that interests you. You respond by walking up to the person, a bold action on your part. Yet, your approach lacks any enthusiasm or energy. After getting the persons attention with a "Hello", you proceed with the following: "I think you are attractive and I'd like to get to know you. I must tell you though, I don't know who I am, why I am here or where I'm going."

Where would you expect the conversation to go from here?

Is your expectation that the person will respond with overwhelming enthusiasm?

A quotation from Claude Bristol says,
"Thoughts attract that upon which they are directed."

Do not settle for less than what you might become. "Our outer circumstances are the direct results of our inner attitude. By the thoughts we choose -- consciously and unconsciously -- we author the circumstances in our lives. Man is the only known creature who can reshape and remold himself by altering his attitude."(James Allen)

In scripture it is written, "As a man thinkest is heart, so is he."(Proverbs 23:7)

Messages received through out a lifetime are stored, creating the excess baggage hidden in the subconscious. It is these thoughts that limit your activities. Ever had the following experience:

You decide to run out to the grocery store, just for a minute, so you don't put your face on? Some of you are out raged or disgusted with even the suggestion but let's say you do. Your plan is to get in and out as quickly as possible, right? Wrong. Wouldn't you know it? You run into someone that wants to make conversation. It may even be someone you've had your eye on for sometime. Imagine your behavior right now. How are you standing? Are you smiling? Are you creating interesting conversation? No, Why not? Is your perception, the image you have of yourself, controlling your response? Are you responding differently from your normal pattern? Are you usually bubbly and outgoing? What happened? Your automatic responses, personality and behavior, in various situations, are based on the image you have of yourself. It is true that if you believe, you can achieve but any permanent change must occur as a result of inner work. A change in your perception of yourself begins in your subconscious. Subconscious messages that have been aptly coined by someone as "**Sub Mess**."

▲ What sub mess has guided you life?
   What unanswered questions have aided in the development of your self-image?
   Where did the original messages come from?

111

How has your excess baggage influenced your search for love?
Your search to fill the HOLE in your soul?

Ask yourself:

Are you tired of living out of a suitcase packed in your childhood?
That excess baggage that you carry from relationship to relationship?
Who packed your baggage?

Parents (grand)	peers
Teachers	siblings
Clergy	family

Review your PAST.
How long did your relationships last? How did they end?
Are you still friends?
How often have you chosen someone who
clearly was not for you?
Were your expectations realistic, reactive or inappropriate?
To break free, it is necessary to bring the subconscious thoughts conscious. **Speak the messages aloud.** Write them down if it will help. Speaking the messages aloud or writing them down allows your conscious mind to realize how impaired and illogical the messages really are. Unless you come to terms with your past (your pattern), you will continually re-create, in each new relationship, the same results. Until you become aware of the need to break the pattern, you will continually attract the wrong kind of man. If your childhood messages silenced you on things that mattered and you learned not to express feelings, that pattern is carried into your adult relationships. Martin Luther King Jr. proclaimed that "Life begins to end, the moment you become silent about things that matter."

With time, the habitually established behaviors increase the difficulty of being who you were created to be.

112

Pastor Joseph Garlington, Pastor of Covenant Community of Pittsburgh, expressed during a sermon, how easy it is to share only surface feelings. He provided the example of someone asking you a frequently asked question, "How are you?" Though you feel your whole world is caving in, you send out the Hologram and respond, "Fine." When there is no form of expression or outlet for feelings, where do those emotions go? Underground into the subconscious mind. The thoughts become the excess baggage that is carried from relationship to relationship. The result of storing unfinished business is automated behaviors.

Women who remain in emotionally void relationships aid their survival by cutting off a part of self. To protect self, painful emotions are no longer acknowledged, at a conscious or subconscious level. When painful experiences do not have an outlet of expression, the anesthesia of the memory is applied. It is easy then to wear a mask to disguise real emotions. They are buried deep and covered with the dirt of the experience. To dig for them is to re-live the sadness but you must uncover them. You will learn to grow through the knowledge and will not be destined to repeat it.

Growing up as a P.K. or Preacher's kid, the search for self was a continual source of personal struggle. My identification as the Pastor's daughter, a label I wore proudly, obscured my individuality. On most occasions when references were made of me, it took the form of, "Oh, that the Pastor's daughter." It was as if my name was insignificant. With the title came the stereotypical expectations of how I was to act and who I was to be. It was only after years of rebellion, and the development of my career and expertise within my field, that I received acknowledgment of my own personage. One such occasion stands out in my memory. While being honored at an event, I overheard someone say to my father, "So, you're Ilinda' father." As I turned away, I smiled deep inside. My dad, not missing the significant of what had just occurred, smiled when he later shared his delight in acknowledgment of the transformation.

Change can only occur when you first make a commitment to self. A commitment to self, to life and to love. It is to learn to love and appreciate yourself. It was Oscar Wilde that said,

"To love oneself is the beginning of a lifelong romance."

One must take responsibility for his or her own happiness. Margaret Mead, anthropologist, once said, "In the N.Y. Harbor, along with the statue of liberty, there should be a statue of responsibility. Without responsibility there can be no freedom.

Gregory Jaynes quoted Alice Walker in Life magazine, "Don't wait around for other people to be happy for you. Any happiness you get, you've got to make your self."

A question often asked by women at the conclusion of a workshop, is "How have you been able to become a confident, independent woman? The questions are based on the final results they see standing before them. What happened that resulted in a marked change in both appearance and my sense of self worth is not a story that can be told in a paragraph or two.

Suffering from the same handicapping condition as most women, that of low self-esteem, I struggled with trying desperately to please. As a child, it was my peers, parents, teachers or anyone within my immediate environment. As an adult, the mission became to please my husband. I gave him the power to cause me to feel small, insignificant, inadequate and undesirable apart from him. Any change had to occur in the perception I held of myself. For me, it required years of hard work, to begin the developmental process of getting to know me. In the evaluative process, in an attempt to regain control of my life, I had to probe into what made Ilinda tick? I had to make a commitment to learn to value self and be willing to fight for my own happiness. It was to stand on the declaration that, "If I make myself happy then I know at least one person is happy." It was not an easy task and if attempted, you can find yourself unconsciously slipping back into the familiar. The familiar includes the negative messages you received and stored as part of your design. You've believed the lies.

Consequently, you like I often do not recognize how much you have going for you.

Take a quick inventory and try to put a value on the assets you possess. Eliminate any material or external possession from the list. Write down what makes you uniquely you. Bring to mind the characteristics and qualities that only exist **inside** of you. You ask, "how can I be unique when someone, somewhere has the same quality?" Understand, you have a unique combination of inner qualities that are not exactly duplicated in anyone else. An article in the Times magazine, addressed the subject of cloning and asked the question, "Will There Ever Be Another You?" The answer involved several pages yet the answer was simply: NO. Projecting into the future or searching into the ancient archives of the past will not produce a carbon copy or clone of an exact you.

Someone once penned that "man lives in unconscious imitation of each other, then wonders why they are uncomfortable with themselves".

In a world of individuals, comparing oneself to another is a futile activity.

A positive approach is to accept your self, as you are now, though your are not all you hope to be. It is to begin to change what you can and accept what cannot be. Positive self-acceptance is to not allow society to define or dictate who you are. It is to sacrifice the time needed to discover the answers that only you can supply. Anne Morrow Linbergh in her book, *Gift from the Sea*, reflects that "women are taught to give where it is needed- and immediately. The results are the spilling and giving of self away to the thirsty, while seldom being allowed the time to let the pitcher fill up to the brim." (Paraphrased)

Take the time. Work on yourself everyday. Understanding yourself and recognizing the gifts that are within you will give you the confidence and inner peace you seek.

The following poem aptly expresses the above conviction:
Don't prejudge me with your point of view,
I am the woman you wished you knew,
Don't be fooled by what you see,
Beauty and grace are just a part of me.
This is just a body, in which my Spirit resides,

115

There is more to me,
The best is inside.

The Virtuous Woman

An excellent (virtuous) wife (woman), who can find? For her
worth is far above jewels,
The heart of her husband trusts in her, and he will have no lack of
gain.
She does him good and not evil all the days of her life.
Proverbs 31:10 -- 12 (New American Standard)

Do you want to be the woman that people seek after? You
know the one that everyone wants to include in his or her social
events? Do you want to be sought after by men versus being the
seeker, then become a virtuous woman. The description of the
virtuous woman, written in the best selling book ever, the Bible,
sounds like a 90's woman. She appears to be vibrant and full of
life. Let's follow her path.

She saves money for the family by sewing her own clothes.
She enjoys cooking gourmet foods (brings her food from afar) and
she gets up early, while it is still night to prepare it for her family
including her servants. The virtuous woman purchases land to start
her own business (entrepreneur), increasing her potential for profit.
She is community minded and gets involved with projects
benefiting the poor. Talk about the juggling act, she is successful
in balancing work and family, she does it all. Her family is seen in
the finest styles of clothing (reds, purples, and fine linen) and she
still has time to be supportive of her husband of status. AND she
smiles at the future.

Whew! You are probably hyperventilating by now and
thinking a number of things. Even with the advantages and
assistance of modern technology many are most likely saying:

- Never mind, I' ll sit this one out.
- If it takes all of that, I am not doing it.
- That does not sound like a 90's woman to me

116

You are right about that one. The modern tech woman would be described as working outside the home and not juggling the balls well. In fact, she may drop a few by not cooking, sewing (most certainly not) or knowing where the children are. Husband? Huh, he is on his own. He can do for himself. The modern gadgets utilized to make work easier were created to create time. Time to relax and enjoy family yet what has been the effect?

Maybe the amount of activity overwhelms you but more importantly, let us not miss the attributes of the virtuous woman's character. She exhibits:

Strength

Dignity

And Wisdom

Kindness fills her mouth.

She operates with integrity because she fears (reverence) the Lord. If she says she will do it (what ever it is), her word becomes her bond. You can depend on her to be there. As a result of being an excellent woman, her mate can trust her with his heart. Can you even imagine being with someone that you can share your heart with and trust they will handle with care? What a liberating feeling that must be. No, wonder her mate praises her saying, "Baby, you are the best, far above all others." (Paraphrase)

"If you have anything really valuable to contribute to the world, it will come through the expression of your own personality—that single spark of divinity that sets you off and makes you different from every other living creature." Bruce Barton

In the October 1996 Issue of Black Woman, an article titled, *What He Wants In A Wife*, included the desire of Brian, an artist manager. His desire is to have someone whom he could trust fully and openly with his deepest feelings. He stated, "I need to depend on her no matter what the circumstances and she'll be there for me through thick and thin."

You may be remarking, "I wish I had that in a man." Acknowledge and consider the quotation that says: To have a friend you must first be a friend." Anonymous

Become the positive person that operates with integrity and careful thought. Treat everyone you meet with respect and act as if they are the most important person in the moment. The woman, who exhibits the attributes of a virtuous character, is ready to meet a good man, perhaps her mate for a lifetime, if she so chooses. To take it a step further, could be you are no longer searching but attempting to maintain the relationship you are in. Speak with kindness and be a virtuous woman to your mate. If you again respond with, "I am not doing that" then look over your shoulder and pay attention to **WHO'S SLIPPING IN YOUR BACK DOOR.**

HOW TO

KEEP IT

IF YOU GOT

IT

CHAPTER 6

WHO'S SLIPPIN IN YOUR BACK DOOR

Midwestern minister received a thank you note from a bridegroom that he had recently joined in marriage. This is what he wrote:

"Dear Reverend,

I want to thank you for the beautiful way you brought my happiness to a conclusion."

It was probably not what he meant yet sadly it often proves to be truth. The prevailing thought amongst the general populous is that marriage *is* the beginning of the end. To many, it represents the end of a person's freedom, happiness, and all that symbolizes life. One may even sarcastically pose the question, "Is there life after marriage?"

All one has to do to confirm the popular belief (regarding marriage) is to listen. Listen to the jokes a groom endures when announcing his intentions to marry. It is popular etiquette to congratulate the female and to tell the groom "good luck." His fiancée' is referred to as "the old ball and chain" by his friends. They facetiously project the image of his walking mindlessly around the mall, following his soon-to-be bride, while carrying her purse. Not a pretty picture, is it? Someone even suggested that once a man gets down on one knee, he never gets back up. While it is truth that not all marriages end when they begin, it appears that a greater percentage fails. Current statistics indicate that one out of two or 50% of those that create a paper trail (by obtaining a marriage certificate) fail. Jackie Mason, comedian, posed a poignant question when he asked, "Why do people still get married with the rate of failed marriages? Would you invest in a business with such a record of failure?

When asked the happiness quotient of their marriage, couples tend to infer satisfaction. Yet the same couple often exists, unaware of the dangerous status of their marriage.

How does this happen? The movie, **Waiting To Exhale**, created from the book by the same title, by author Terry McMillian, seems to illustrate what occurs. Prior to finding, selecting, and committing to a mate, a person is figuratively holding her breath in anticipation. They are waiting to exhale. From my observances, it appears that once they marry, the pressure is released and they both exhale. The male exhales and daily increases the amount of body fat and muscles (in the relaxed state) his body contains. The female, after having exhaled, begins to think nothing of going out in public in hair rollers and a scarf. Wearing flannel pajamas to bed becomes the norm and sleeping in the buff is virtually a figment of someone's imagination. After all, why should one do, what one did in order to get him, to keep him? Is it not okay to relax? To just be yourself?

If the above thoughts symbolize your present behavior, ask yourself the following:

▲ How has my behavior changed from the relationship's inception?

When did I stop doing the things that keep the relationship alive and vibrant?

Were there caring things I used to do for him that I no longer do?

Why did I stop?

Is it that I really believe that it (whatever it is) is unnecessary to enjoy a happy marriage or was time the enemy?

One Sunday morning my father, Pastor Lawrence Boone, told of a conversation between a husband and a wife as they rode in their car. The wife began the conversation by asking the question, "Do you remember when I used to sit next to you while riding in the car?" The husband replied with a shrug, Yeah." She continued her line of questioning as she hugged the door. "Do you remember how close we used to be?" "Yeah," he answered quietly. After a few silent moments she asked, "What happened?" Without looking in her direction, he answered, "You moved."

The distance between two people requires only one person to move. The driver of the car in this illustration, the husband, by all outward appearances remanded stationary. The conversation implies that the wife, having stopped doing what she used to do, was unwilling to take responsibility for the deterioration of the relationship.

However, with closer examination, a few questions may shed a different light on the state of affairs.

When did she move?

Was it gradual or progressive?

Did he notice when she moved?

Did his conversation or actions prompt her to move?

Is he comfortable with where she is? If not, why did he not request her to return to her former position?

Of course, you cannot answer questions regarding an anonymous couple but how about a few personal ones?

Do your own evaluation of a present or recent relationship (memory still fresh?)

Perhaps this application will be more applicable to those that are married. Attempt to reflect and answer the following:

▲ Are there caring things that you used to do that you no longer do? Certainly.

- When did you stop

- Holding hands?

- Wearing that something special he enjoys seeing you in?

- Working at looking good just for him, fixing your hair or applying makeup?

- Feeling a sexual charge when he enters the room?

- Sitting in the circumference of his armpit?

- Smiling and enjoying his conversation or laughing at his not-so-funny jokes? You know the ones you used to giggle hysterically about?

- Gazing sensuously into his eyes as if looking deep into his soul?

- Are you in one part of the house while he is in another?

When was the last time.....

- You gave your partner a full-body massage?

- Paid for a night at a local hotel?

- Had a meaningful conversation with no interruptions?

When did you lose your ability to play? To play together with non-sexual motives? Playing successfully involves openness and trust, without the end goal of sex. Ever known a couple who began a pillow fight, laughing and wrestling, and ended up in an angry confrontation? It sometimes resulted in a physical fight. Doesn't sound like anyone you know, right?

More questions. Inquiring minds want to know:

When did your relationship get so serious? Or mundane?

Are you in a rut?

A rut is just a grave with both ends knocked out. Perhaps you find yourself doing the same things, the same way, with the same person, at the same time every day. Sounds like a rut to me, how about you? Pastor Warren Weirsbe puts it this way, "I know love is blind, but search 'til you find, a face you can stand, everyday."

A couple of lines from the song, *After the Love is Gone,* illustrates the road taken by many couples. The words say, "Something happened along the way, we used to be happy, now we're sad...for awhile to love each other was all we needed...."

"But there are explanations," you say (protesting loudly in your own defense). "Our conversations are boring. We have nothing to talk about. We know everything there is to know about each other." A motivational speaker once said, "You are bored because you are boring." Still with me?

Then visualize this scenario:

You and your mate go out to your favorite restaurant. Do you look at the menu and without consulting your mate, place their order? Of course not, you respond indignantly. Why not? Because you do not know what he wants? Or why does he ask you if you know each other so well? Why don't you order for him the same thing he always orders? How about ordering even what he had the last time he came to this particular restaurant? His desires and interest change with time? Really? You don't say? Hmmm?

Over time, a couple begins the gradual process that allows them to take each other for granted. It is to assume they know everything there is to know about the other. A.W. Tozer pointed out that the "Stars are seen every clear night. If one only saw the stars once every 1,000 years, would not the stars be a special event?"

Perhaps you are guilty of thinking, "He will always be there." The negativism represented in this statement is one of the symptoms of a terminal illness infecting many marriages. The negative force begins when the relationship, whether new or mature, begins to succumb to sameness. It is when you no longer find a need to explore, with the wonderment of a child, your mate. You know the phrase, "Familiarity breeds contempt?"

Kahilga Braums penned a beautiful love poem that asked, "How do I love thee? Let me count the ways." How many ways can you count?

Take a moment (or as long as you need) to list the ways you love your mate.

Difficult task? Only needed a few moments? Had not thought about it for a while? Can you remember when you stopped counting? Probably not. It happens so gradually that the moment is missed.

The chains of habit are illustrated in a familiar quotation that says, "The chains of habit are too weak to be felt until they are too strong to be broken."

Has it become habit to only see the dark side of the man you claim to love? Does your negative frame of mind focus on the qualities you have recorded as wrong? It is said that "After marriage, a woman's sight can become so keen that she can see right through her husband without looking at him and a man's sight can become so dull that he can look right at his wife without seeing her."

Dr. James Dobson encourages you to, "Keep your eyes wide open before marriage, and half shut afterwards." It is said that no one judges anyone as harshly as married couples judge each other.

Again the question:
When did your relationship get in trouble? It is not in trouble you say? No? Do you continue to hurt each other out of innocence or ignorance? Are you prepared to take off the rose-colored glasses you have been wearing and do a reality check?

Ask yourself:

▲ Are you still the joy of his life?

Does his soul yearn for you in the night, as the writer of

Isaiah 26:9 wrote?

In the morning does his spirit soar because of you? Or are you a bore?

A few additional questions may provide the litmus test needed to determine if you are:

How does he react when you ask for a cold glass of water after he sat down or got into bed?

While at work, he has the opportunity and access to a telephone, does he call you?

You are going out at night. Does he express his concern for your safety by reminding you to lock your doors or does he ask you to bring something back for him?

Realizing the above actions can also be done by rote or out of routine, only you can perceive if he responds with delight to your request.

A reoccurring, familiar theme is the feeling that the fire and passion have gone out. Couples who are experiencing the opposite of a passion-filled connection. Your mate does not request intimacy and it seems to always be your idea or it does not happen. His priorities appear to have shifted and you are experiencing a feeling of rejection. Where does one begin (again) to rekindle the flame?

"A marriage may be made in heaven but the maintenance must be done on earth. (Anonymous)

Is your retort, "Naw, you **do not** understand. There are things that have come between us."

Are things more important than the person is?

If asked the reasons for marital discourse, the list, from a cross section of people, will usually include:

Money (# 1)

Irreconcilable Differences

Loss of Love

Consider a few additional factors that contribute to the deterioration of a relationship. Let's look at the cold water that may have put out the fire.

1. Neglect

A case for neglect occurs when you allow yourself to become caught up in the activities of life: work, family systems, religious activities, and much more. It results in your having little inclination, time, or energy to devote to the relationship. The business (busy ness) of life becomes all too consuming. The aforementioned activities are important but should not take the attention from one's mate.

An anonymous writer stated that "love thrives in the face of all life's hazards, save one—neglect."

Holy wedlock does not become holy deadlock overnight. No one married with the thought of how soon can we be divorced. Couples do not come together and agree on a conscious plan to destroy the marriage. It is the slow erosion that eats at the roots, not the big things that erode the relationship. Like the oak tree that survives the winds of the storms yet is felled by tiny beetles that ate at its roots. The damage is beneath the surface, unseen to the natural eye and it proves to be deadly. Robert Gordon Menzies, author of The Measure of Years, when he said, "More good things in life are lost by indifference than ever were lost by active hostility" seldom speak truer words than those.

Have you ever experienced hearing that a couple was getting a divorce and you went into immediate shock? Why? For all intent and purposes, they appeared to be happy. No one suspected the disease that daily ate at the roots of their marriage.

Your mate is dying by degrees and you are not even aware of it. *until* he lets his imagination roam.

2.   Open Hostility

Perhaps you are antagonized by the problems within the relationship and become openly hostile in actions and deeds. Most readers shiver to think of the position of the man who is the target of such hostility. A woman on a mission. The female who makes it a common practice to embarrass her mate in public. As the avenger approaches, those in the vicinity hear her theme song that represents her intent, "Do not get mad, just get even."

As one seeking retaliation, you are prepared for head-to-head combat. Your words are no longer spoken out of kindness (or even with the same politeness with which you would greet a stranger) but with animosity. Your words are filled with years of resentment, bitterness and anger.

You exhibit a terminal negativism and you make no apologies for spreading the infection.

Being unwillingly included in conversations of this nature, between couples, I have often observed such attacks. The embarrassment of the male, the object of the vindictive, vicious attack, was obvious to everyone but the female. Maybe the safety in numbers rule spurred on her use of hurtful words. I will never know the motivating factors. I do not go home with them. Perhaps if you were the observer of this particular situation, you might try to redirect the conversation. Unsuccessfully, I might add. After a few moments of attempting to play defense attorney, to help the one being attacked save face, I usually look for an escape hatch.

It reminds me of the words of Robert Fulghum, author of *All I Really Need to Know I Learned In Kindergarten:* "Sticks and stones may break our bones, but words will break our hearts."

A story is told of a man who was asked, in the absence of his wife, "How old is your wife?" "Eighty-seven" he answered, "God willing she will live to be 100." How old are you? came the next question. "Eighty-seven and hopefully I'll live to be 101." Curiosity got the best of the questioner, so he asked. "Why would you say you want to live to be 101 years of age and your wife to live to 100?" He replied quietly, "To tell you the truth, I would like just one year of peace before I die."

The echo of Celeste Holm's words, "We live by encouragement and we die without it—slowly, sadly, angrily."

Even when a half-hearted effort is made to be playful, women feel free, through sarcasm, to take pot shots at their men. Their comments include such verbiage as:

"You dog. You worthless piece of Sh--"

You probably noticed the pronoun was changed from "you" to the more general term, "women." This was done not without notice but to relieve the pressure you may have begun to feel if you are guilty. Let's go further.

Ever watch or participate in a conversation when a male is relating an incident and his wife is present? As the male continually attempts to finish his story, make his point, or contribute to the conversation, his mate repeatedly interrupts. She may frequently invalidate him by saying, "You're wrong. Or you're crazy." Then speaking to the others present, "He doesn't know what he's talking about. It's like this..."The words used may not be the same but his words are never heard. He never gets in a word.

This brings to mind the story of a judge who sternly eyed a man standing before him. He said, "Your wife charges you with not having spoken to her in five years. What is your explanation, he asked?" "Well Your Honor," replied the man, "I didn't think it was polite to interrupt her." Not true you say?

Try this experiment:

▲ Ask your partner to relate to you the last conversation the two of you had that he can remember. Ask him if he felt you actually heard and understood him? He will probably drop his newspaper at the mere hint of interest. Can he remember what was said or done that gave him a sense of your presence? This experiment may lead to a continual discussion of what behaviors created the

130

perception that you were or were not listening. In any case, the exercise can open up interesting dialogue.

From Dr. Charles Swindoll's commentary come the following the quotation, "If your marriage is failing, maybe it's because your mate is dying from lack of encouragement, lack of affirmation, lack of respect, but most of all from the lack of grace, grace that only you can give."

An illustration comes to mind and it describes a woman that talked incessantly. When her marriage became troubled, she and her husband agreed to attend counseling sessions. At the first session, the woman began talking. After a lengthy period of time the counselor said he would like to hear the husband's side of the story. The wife replied, "Oh I know. When I get done telling you my side, I'll tell you his side."

Still do not believe your relationship is in trouble? Sometimes not facing the truth about your relationship allows someone to sneak in a door you did not know you left open.

So, Who Is She?

The name is not important.

A current magazine recently reported 75% of the married men that have affairs never leave their wives. It also reports 40% of adults are unfaithful to their mates within their lifetime. (Orlando Sentinel, 1995) Women, who are attracted to and date only married men, do so to avoid commitment. Their objective, similar to that of a percentage of single men, is a low maintenance association. It would be stretching it to call it a relationship. The attraction faction is little implied commitment. An article in the February 1993 Issue of Ebony Man labeled women who seek to become involved with married men only as gold-diggers. Gold-diggers theorize that married men take you out when they want to go out, they treat you better, they spend more money on you and when its time, you send them home."

Perhaps, on the surface it appears that the issue is money, but upon closer examination one will discover deeper, unresolved issues. What are the issues?

Why are relationships so vulnerable?

Why is it that someone bright, witty and good-looking or a not-so-attractive woman (by societal standards) of average intelligence can steal your mate?

From Secrets of a Mistress by Rose Smith (think it's her real name), Rose shared these words: "I'm the other woman: seductress, mistress, home wrecker. I can come into your life and abruptly tear apart what you've spent 5, 10 even 25 years building."

"Steal my man," you say, "How dare she make such a statements." More importantly, the question should be, how? How does it happen? What factors contribute to the demise of the marriage?

The following is not offered to excuse the offending party that chooses to taste of the forbidden fruit of another. It is offered to give insight into, an otherwise, common situation yet contributing a different perspective.

Contemplate the scenarios presented earlier in the chapter. While you may not agree, reflect on what is being said before you disagree.

What techniques are used by "the other" woman to capture the heart of your mate?

The other woman notices what is missing in the relationship. She studies your mate and begins the subtle process of supplying what she perceives he needs. Contrary to your usual practice, she smiles when he enters the room and engages him in conversation. She listens attentively, hanging on to his every word. He believes he's after her and before he realizes he's captured.

You can probably recall an occasion when your mate came home excited about something that had occurred during the day.

He wanted to tell the love of his life. You. Can you also recall your responding with a disinterested, "Uh huh." Maybe you made no attempts to even feign excitement. Conversations shared amongst your friends reveal your thought patterns with comments such as, "I don't have time to listen to what he's talking about. Besides, I listened yesterday and what he said then wasn't worth anything then either." Though you may not be listening, the truth is someone is.

Think About It:

▲ Would you continue to share your heart if this was the typical response you received each time you did? Dr. Nathan Hare confirmed, "Men refuse to open up and tell women what they are feeling for fear that women will feel they are weak."

In many instances the assumption is a correct one. Why are men so afraid? To answer the question, let me ask one. It is true you can not answer a question with a question, but here goes. Can you be trusted with his feelings?

After attempting to share with you, does he feel deflated? As if he has been kicked in the stomach? Don't know? Then ask him. After a few blows of such intensity, he will not continue to reveal his emotional need. He starts looking, often subconsciously, for another outlet to fill the need he has. It may be through a male or female friend but it is often

"The other woman."

At this stage of vulnerability, in steps the mistress or the "other woman," whatever your choice or terminology. Come to think of it, your language may not be as kind. However, the other woman recognizes the need and advances toward filling it. Need an example?

Let's say you are sexually conservative, scarcely acknowledging to him that it was good. You may even state, "I do not want to tell him because he may get the big head." SHE, on the other hand, is wonderfully wild. SHE initiates sex and even takes

133

advantage of exploratory positions. SHE lets him know how much she appreciates his skills, techniques and anatomy. While your pessimistic criticism drives the stake deep into his heart, SHE pampers him, giving him that extra attention he longs for. Someone once said, "Sexual infidelities occur, not when someone is looking for sexual adventure, but looking for somebody to say, You're #1."

Perhaps the man you have been married to for 16 years (arbitrary number with no significance except to indicate long term) has not been unfaithful. Though he is not happy with the lovemaking, he never complains. You assume that because he says nothing, he has nothing to say. An erroneous and often dangerous assumption. To a friend he may complain that you never initiate sex. He continues to share with a friend that he gets the sense "she (you) doesn't want it as often."

Even though reports conclude that millions of women do not experience a physical, internal pressure to have sex, he takes it personal. In this case, it is necessary to change his perception of your rejection. Sex, a Spiritual experience, is to be one of the most intimate experiences between two people. Husbands reveal sex is important. With that statement, women all over the world are yelling, "Tell me something I don't know." Women whole heartily agree with the statement and make such comments as, "That's all they think about," or "I could hardly keep his hands off me." The remarks, when made during the dating stage, contain an underlying tone, that of flattery of the pursuit.

The question then becomes:

If women acknowledge the quest and the physical interest of men before entering a relationship, what is expected after the consummation of the relationship?

While attending an Image Projection workshop, the words of the presenter caught me off guard. They seemed unrelated to the topic being presented. The presenter (she) stated, that men think about sex every 11 seconds. The majority of men, when asked for validation of the information supported her analogy. They then
134

added that even between that time, they are thinking. This is not to say they're only thinking about SEX. Certainly not. It is important, but not for the reasons females may have concluded. Men report it is not just for the physical release but for emotional reasons as well. Sex is less about sex and more about who he is. His socialization process has taught him that who he is based on his ability to perform. To quote an anonymous husband, "If we haven't made love in a long time," he told his wife, "then I feel more isolated, not just from you, but from everyone around me."

Another bold statement from Rose Smith, mistress, affirms, "Why, then, if I'm so average, does a married man risk all to have a fling with me?"

Her answer,

"Because I know how to make a man feel. Believe   me, that's not something you can't do in your marriage."

A comment made by a distrustful wife, "I am going to make sure my husband does not cheat on me. That is why I go everywhere he goes. Otherwise I know where he is every minute." How logical is this thought pattern?

Who can know the whereabouts of another individual 24/7? (Translation: 24 hours a day, 7 days a week)

If there is not trust, on what foundation does the relationship rest?

THINK ABOUT IT:

▲   Does holding someone so tightly assure they will be yours exclusively?

Does knowing where they are and with whom, secure your position?

The scenario brings to mind the illustration of the butterfly. Visualize a beautifully colored, rare butterfly. As it happens, you are the proud owner of this precious treasure. You train it to respond to your voice and to land on your hand upon command.

Would it be advantageous to close your hand tightly, to assure its safety and prevent escape? Of course not! Your attempt to contain the butterfly would result in its death. It would not matter that your intentions were to only hold a precious prize close. The results are the same.

Remember, wrestling with a sibling or schoolmate as a child? What happened when they, purely by chance, got the upper hand and pinned you to the floor? Was your response to simply lie there and yell "Surrender?" Probably not, unless it was a manipulative ploy being used to gain an early release. For me, it energized me to struggle even more, to gain the upper hand. My survival depended on how badly I wanted to be free. The tighter my brother's held me, the harder I fought to be free.

What happened if they suddenly stood up and released me? Did I appreciate the release and walk away ending the contest? NOOO! Not really wanting the challenge to end, I then pounced on my contender.

The Actuality? What you hold tightly will ultimately fight to be free. Why continue to use techniques that result in the destruction of the relationship? An anonymous writer advised, "The best way to hold a man is in your arms."

Perhaps you prefer the advice that says, "If you love something let it go and if it is yours it will return to you. If it doesn't, hunt it down and kill it."

When you think of your mate, what degree of trust is there? If there is documented evidence that substantiates your lack of trust, what action will you take?

Will your focus be to increase your attempts to control his behavior?

A magazine article, in response to a Dear Joan type letter, suggested to a woman that she check the speedometer of her mate's car. It further recommended a subtle approach to questioning his activities of the day to confirm what she suspects. I personally prefer the advice from Oprah Winfrey who said, "When you find your self in the car prepared to follow your man (because you don't trust him), drive yourself instead to the hospital. You need help."

136

The statement spoke to the reality of the declaration of the woman who would choose the options listed above. Her comments range from, "Let me tell you, if I catch him, I'll kill him" to "No, I'm going after her."

Why would either be considered an option? It was always intriguing to me, during my high school years, that two females ended up fighting over a male. The question, that always peaked my curiosity was, why were the two females fighting? Did not the male realize whom he preferred? Why was he even given the option to choose?

The same scene is regularly played out on talk shows. Two females, after discovering his indiscretion (evidence in their face -- other female sitting there) are asked, "What do you plan to do?" After a long pause, and an obvious groping for words, they usually respond. Their statements often include an unwillingness to take responsibility and an ambivalent thought pattern that says: "He has to make a decision. Will it be her or me?" And that is where they leave it. They clearly take pride in having made a bold statement of declaration. They never realize (unless an astute audience member or host points it out) that they are simply rationalizing and justifying staying in the relationship.

Trust gives you the ability to rise above your doubts. The foundation of a relationship must rest on trust. If it does not, the ripple effect will be felt in other areas of the relationship. It makes for a miserable existence, not only for the distrustful spouse, but also for all that share their space.

Now do not get defensive. The message frequently received from independent women takes the following form:

"He's not the only one in the situation. I'm not satisfied with the relationship and haven't been in a long time."

Contrary to popular belief, the prevalent response to the question, "Did you tell him" is:

- Why should I have to tell him...

- If I do not feel like it, why...
- Then he is a weak man, let him..

I have other responsibilities now, he can....

All the above statements may be truth but answer a few additional questions:

▲ When did you stop supplying positive reinforcement in regular dosages? Why?

Have you ever faked an orgasm or displayed outward delight when it just was not there?

Why did you do it? To protect his ego?

But things changed. You no longer feel it necessary to be his shield, the protector. In fact, the fiery darts are coming from an internal source. You.

In previous chapters, the underlying reason for your response has been analyzed and explored. Your mental anguish results in your minimizing what is good in the man. Instead of looking at your mate through the eyes of an outsider, **you** develop a wandering eye. You notice that "other man" now looks more appealing than your own. Ask yourself, "Why does this individual look better to me than the one I'm with? Why has the grass started to look greener in the other yard?"

Understandably, you have often heard the above cliche, but follow for a moment the analogy.

Often someone else's lawn does look greener. With closer examination, you discover someone is taking the time to maintain his or her lawn. Along with mowing, they are weeding and watering are done regularly. You see, you are not close enough to see the weeds but they are there.

What is the application to relationships?

How can your mate, a piece of a man (by your own declaration) become someone else's lover? You have become so accustomed to the negative in the man, you fail to realize he still has some good things about him. The good characteristics have

138

gone underground. To rediscover them will require breaking up the hardened surface, tilling the ground, and cultivating the soil (the soul). In some cases, it may be necessary to plant new seed.

Thomas W. McKnight and Robert H. Phillips, authors of *"More Love Tactics*," wrote, "By honing your power of observation you can recognize the things that are going on inside and in his life."

A Healthy Relationship:

What does it look like?
MAYBE YOU *ONCE* HAD IT.... Is Your Marriage Healthy?

Allow me to begin this section with a personal observation. While in the company of a male friend, a female acquaintance casually remarked that she would love to have a body like his. It was not her intent to change her gender. No, her expression was in appreciation of his physical physique. It was in admiration of his 6' 3" statue and perfectly proportioned body. He smiled in acknowledgment as we walked away. The experience immediately brought to mind several observations.

Was she really saying that she was willing to do what was necessary to obtain a physically fit body? Did she even understand what she was saying? Did she have any knowledge of the sacrifice and discipline necessary?

The analogy quickly turned into an application, within my mind, for couples. I reflected on couples that have, what appears to be the type of relationship that everyone desires. Yet most, looking from the outside, are unaware of the discipline and high price the couple has paid to obtain it. Healthy relationships are not devoid of difficulties. The partners view problems as challenges and they continually seek solutions.

Successful couples realize relationships offer a great opportunity for growth through self-discovery.

To evaluate the healthiness of your relationships, Susan Taylor, publisher of *Essence* magazine, poised the following questions:

Are my relationships working? Are they healthy? Constructive? If not, why not? Am I giving what I want to receive? Healthy relationships know how to balance love, sex and life.

A handout by Kathy Stupka, through the Center for the Prevention of Domestic Violence, presented *Elements of Healthy Relationships.* A few of the recommendations included:

- Allows individuality
- Brings out the best in partner
- Freedom to ask honestly for wants
- Does not attempt to change or control the other person
- Welcomes closeness, risks vulnerability

What makes a good relationship?

A **good relationship** is based on an equal balance of power. The objective is not to control through coercion, money, or sex.

A story is told of a couple starting their marriage on the wrong foot by using power-tripping tactics and sex as a weapon. It occurred on their wedding night, as they prepared to consummate their marriage, that the man slung his pants across the room. They landed on his wife's head. He instructed her to put them on. She replied, "I cannot wear your pants." He answered, "That's right, remember that." She said nothing, went into the rest room and came out in a black negligee. She then threw her panties at her new husband. As he caught them, she said, "Put them on." As he clutched them, he said with an air of confusion, "I cannot get in these." "You're right," she confirmed, "and you won't get in them if you do not change your attitude."

In a **healthy relationship**, each has a concern for and is sensitive to the needs and feelings of the other. It is shared power, with neither seeking to dominate the other. It exhibits itself in a "we" thinking pattern, not a "me" focus. Healthy couples recognize that what affects one person will affect both.

Most importantly, a healthy couple can rely on one another without requiring the other to be a life support system. Both partners are able to stand alone while together. Joe Murray, Cox News service represents a healthy relationship in the statement below, "Marriage should be a duet: When one sings, the other claps."

As established earlier, healthy relationships are difficult and challenging. From an anonymous source comes the following clarification:

"When two people are involved a relationship, there are actually six people involved:

The person we think we are

The person our partner thinks we are

The person we believe our partner thinks we are

The person our partner thinks he or she is

The person we think our partner is

The person our partner believes we think he or she is". The author of the above exposition believes there are possibly 50 possible relationships within one. This explanation presents a new insight into Rodney King's question, "Can't we all just get along?" John Kendrick Bangs voiced, "It is necessary to be almost a genius to make a good husband."

Unhealthy relationships leave one broken and needing healing.

After assessing your relationship, you may discover you have stayed too long. The justification and rationalization often includes not having the financial freedom to leave, fear of the unknown, or staying for the children. Individuals in unhealthy relationships are often heard telling their mate, "You know my children come first." In most instances, the children were born to both of them. The observations were generally women, (though I am aware of a few exceptions), who believe they cannot take a vacation or go out with their mate because of the children. It is as if, once the children arrived, they needed care and the marriage did not.

Whether the decision is to stay or leave, acknowledging that mistakes were made is the first step to recovery.

How to Affair-Proof Your Relationship

This section does not come with a money-back guarantee nor does it contain a disclaimer. Because of the variables associated with every coupling, a person may work all the steps and their mates still cheat. The implication is not that you are responsible for the actions of another. The observations listed, are techniques used by successful couples and have seemed to work. The information is offered as proven recommendations. The application and customization of the information requires your participation.

So, what can you do to affair-proof your relationship?

Do what is necessary to arouse the love that once burned like a consuming fire. The goal of marriage is to renew continually the love for one person.

After 50 years of marriage, Henry Ford replied, "I've treated marriage like I've made automobiles -- just stick to one model."

The maintenance of a marriage requires, no, demands, a willingness to work hard at it. A quotable saying from an anonymous source says, "We did not guess that love would prove so hard a master."

Love Is As Love Does

In a previous chapter, the needs of the male gender were indicated. However, purposely the greatest need of a man was not mentioned. It was withheld for inclusion in this chapter. Though the aforementioned are important, a man has a greater need for Honor and Respect from his mate. It is commanded, in scripture, that "the husband must love, the wife must respect." Ephesians. 5:33)

So you say, "I respect my mate." Internally this may be true, but externally how is it demonstrated?

Love is not what it says; it is what it does. Remember?

142

This simple yet profound phrase contained in the movie, *Forest Gump,* spoken by Tom Hanks began the development of thought for me. It was not until Minister Adrian Wilson (clergy of Covenant Community), repeated the phrase during a Sunday morning service, that my thoughts began to flow. Love Is as Love Does. What is love? What does love do? What does love look like? It looks like what it does.

When you begin to evaluate, can this marriage be saved, contemplate what of value remains. With the maturity of the marriage, when all that is left are the memories, what will you have to remember? Will there be meaningful events that cause you to smile even then when you look back?

If you conclude that the relationship is worth saving, ponder the following on *How to keep it if you got it.* The observations offered below have been reported to work by couples that have successfully maintained their relationship. The knowledge, gathered from many sources, will help you to lock the back door, securing it with a dead bolt.

*   **Commitment**

A high level of commitment is often not exhibited within the reality of today's relationships. Large portions are even unwilling to enter into a marriage contract, legalizing and legitimizing the bond. To be committed is represented by the determination to build, provide, and protect the relationship. There is a commitment to spend time.

An anonymous writer created a credo to be read by couples, willing to make a commitment to each other. A credo is an established mode of speech, a creed or formula.

The following is an excerpt of the promise:

A CREDO

You and I are in a relationship that I value and want to keep. Yet each of us is a separate person with his own unique needs and the right to meet those needs.

143

When you are having problems meeting your needs, I will try to listen with genuine acceptance in order to facilitate your finding your own solution instead of depending on mine. I also will try to respect your right to choose your own beliefs and develop your own values, different though they may be from mine.

...At those times when we find that either of us cannot change his behavior to meet the other's need, let us acknowledge that we have a conflict-of-needs that requires resolving. Let us then commit ourselves to resolve each such conflict without either of us resorting to the use of power or authority to try to win at the expense of the other's losing. I respect your needs, but I also must respect my own...neither will lose, both will win.

*   **Communication**

It is my contention that the major reason for the failure of a marriage is the couples' inability to communicate. The lack of communication may have developed over time or may have never existed (or been established from the relationships' inception). Make your needs clear by expressing them. Do not expect him to guess and then point an accusatory finger when he misses the ever so subtle hints you threw in his direction.

Don't have anything pleasant to talk about? The advice is the same as to the singles. Become interested in your mate and genuinely attentive to his words. For your mate, it will be refreshing to have someone willing to listen. "Most men prefer a listening ear to an agreeing voice." (God's Little Instruction Book)

The scripture advises: "Let no corrupt communication proceed out of your mouth, but that which is good to use of edifying, that it may minister grace unto the hearers"(to benefit those who listen.) Ephesians 4:29.

And listen they will when your words are laced with kindness. Someone once insightfully wrote, "The last word of an argument is what a wife says. Anything the husband says after that is the beginning of another argument."

Josh Billings believes and points out that, "Men are entitled to their opinion as long as is agrees with ours."

How many women ask for a mate's opinion and then actually respect it? This is especially difficult for the strong, independent woman who believes she knows the answer before she asks the question. If the male does not co-sign her direction of thought or has another opinion, whoops! Wrong answer.

When a couple determines what its style or established mode of conversation will be before conflict occurs, a reminder from the partner will often lead to a calmer level of discussion. Conflict is a natural result of two people attempting to communicate their needs. It is simply two opposing thoughts, which require discussion for resolve. When conflict becomes necessary, (and it will) remember the words of Doogie Howser, a television personality from a program of the same name, which reminds one that, "Sometimes the heaviest moment requires the lightest touch." I have discovered a sense of humor always helps. A sense of humor serves as a useful tool when the conversation is set on a collision course.

Someone once said, "When real love exists and a partner is late, schedules overwhelms or careers distract, their time together is used to celebrate. The relief is of being together again, not blaming the other for being absent."

The above statement is a deep thought and principle of operation. I wish I had said it.

When conflict occurs, it is important to focus on fixing the problem, not placing the blame. Focusing on the future does not excuse nor ignore the past. Yesterday's evidence does not equal today's realities. **Let me break it down a bit more for clarification.** Yesterday's evidence may document that he was irresponsibly late but today is today. I was always one who prided myself on my ability to hold a grudge for a long period of time. My reputation said, "Once you crossed me, there was hell to pay." The price I paid, while seeking revenge for yesterday, was empty, wasted years. Looking back did not allow me to look forward. To

145

be free to love is to be able to quickly empathize and apologize for wrongs.

"To err is human, to forgive divine." Shakespeare

Within healthy love, you make allowances for your mate, believing in the ultimate good within that individual. It is having faith in your mate's intentions, though the outcome speaks another language. It is believing in the messenger when the message being broadcast is not clear.

Before speaking, formulate your criticism into a positive format. Rather than saying, "You always forget the dates that should be important," recall for him how much you enjoyed the activity or gift from an occasion he did remember.
Point of illustration:

> Your mate goes to the store and takes what seems like an inordinate amount of time to return.
> What thought patterns do you follow?
> Do you jump to the conclusion that he stopped somewhere else?
> Does your voice take an accusatory tone the moment he steps through the door?
> Do you respond to your assumptions or his explanation?
> Is an explanation even necessary?

While a member of a training organization, ITC (International Training in Communication), I learned a model for providing constructive instructions. The technique learned through ITC trains the individual to utilize the system to: commend, recommend, and commend. The ideal is to learn to sandwich criticism between layers of praise. It is to always provide more positive feedback than negative, complimenting your man. Most importantly, learn to praise in public and reserve criticism for private moments. He may be very wrong but why display your dirty laundry for everyone to see? Fortune 500 companies have successfully adopted similar practices when managing people.

A lack of results from the negative response can be demonstrated by watching the behavior of spouses on talk shows.

146

They believe they are helping their mate to change by: belittling, name calling, and ridiculing.

*   **Thoughtful Gestures**

My observation of a happily married couple includes: his getting up early enough to go to the coffee shop to purchase his wife a doughnut before they depart for work. Not required but what do you think this daily ritual says to her?

- Protect your time together

- Establish your priorities

- Enjoy each other's company.

- Establish a time that is set aside just for the two of you and protect it.

Place it on your schedule and write it in ink in your appointment book. Treat it as you would a dentist appointment or any other high priority. If asked by someone to schedule and appointment during that slot, simply respond, "No, I already have an appointment. Let's look at another time." Your mate will perceive that he is a priority and an important person in your life. When your time as a couple must give way to every task, major or incidental, the relationship becomes a secondary event.

*   **Stroke the passion and keep the fire burning**

Take the initiative to be sexy. If he enjoys making love in the morning, then make love in the morning. Make an unexpected, provocative move. Don't wait until 11:00 p.m. (or whatever the hour) when you are so exhausted you cannot even feign excitement. Take the responsibility to initiate making love. Responsibility means simply the "ability to respond." The tendency is to wait for the male to initiate, stimulate, and conjugate then to consummate. We then wait and anticipate his congratulatory comments on a job well done.

Put another way, comedian Dana Carvey said, "The goal of marriage is to keep lust alive."

Fight against the routine. Ever consider having sex in a secluded area of the beach or in a cabin in front of the fireplace? How about in the middle of the afternoon? Wouldn't hear of it, you say? Did that when your love was young? Perhaps your response leaves clues as to why the fire went out. Visit your local bookstore and pick up a few books on. How to Please Your Mate. There are several on the market. Attend sessions conducted for couples, by couples, that provide real, honest answers to life's challenges. One such group called Couples for Christ, conducted by Covenant Community of Cleveland, holds sessions once each month. Their sessions are lively, animated, and real. There are many marriage enrichment and encounter groups available. Invest in keeping the passion alive. A prayer of affirmation may be a good way for a couple to end a difficult day.

"Lord, where we are wrong, make us willing to change; where we are right make us easy to live with."

The Reverend Peter Marshall

From Melvyn Kinder and Conell Cowan, *Husbands and Wives,* comes the following summary statement: "It takes two people to have a marriage, but only one is necessary to change it...As we abandon our attempts to change our mate and instead focus on ourselves, change surprisingly and predictably occurs in the marriage."

The goal of marriage is to move from the me focus to the we focus. It is to believe in your hopes and dreams. It is to recognize and support the other's hidden talent and potential, while pursuing your own. It is to order your behavior so it contributes the utmost to the growth of the individual and the relationship. A healthy relationship creates a connection between two individuals, which cannot be easily broken.

Advice for scripture says, "Love covers a multitude of sins. I Peter 4:8

My prayer for you as a couple is reflected in the sentiment of an anonymous author who wrote, "I have great hopes that we shall love each other all of our lives as much as if we never married at all."

12

CHAPTER 7

EXPRESSIONS FROM A FROG OR PRINCE:

YOU DECIDE

While in conversation with a female associate and best friend, I again heard the words expressed by the general populace of women. The expression was there are no good men around. The myth is based on the assumption that a "Good Man" is hard to find. Frequently, reports' state that the good ones are either married, in jail, or gay. Gay? Yes, you know you have heard women express to other females the sentiment, "That is a waste of a good man." In response to my friend, I began to look within my immediate environment, with the goal of identifying "Good Men." The result is the location of twelve, who are classified as "Good Men" (according to the working definition established in previous chapters) and were willing to share their side of the story. There were others that did not make this edition but will be included in the future. The names have not been changed to protect the anonymous.

The objective of this chapter is to give Good Men a voice and a forum to speak out on issues important to them. You see Good Men do not make headlines. They are not often invited to be a guest on daytime talk shows. They are not invited to talk about the characteristics of a good man or how to maintain a good, loving relationship with a woman. The topic does not seem to be good for television ratings. Many good men never betray a love by being unfaithful or abusive. As previously stated, to be good by definition, does not mean they are perfect. It does invalidate the categorization of all men. Men, as well as women, should be judged individually and the majority should not be judged by the actions of a few. Men, as women, are to be judged on their individual merit, not by stereotypes.

The following pages are a compilation of men from various walks of life. Although their marital status and positions are unimportant, information included in their individual entries may indicate their present qualifying factors. They hold a variety of positions and some are single while others are married. When asked their opinion, most men will quickly reply, "I am not your typical male." They are probably right. Who is typical and how are the guidelines established? There are few people that can live within a limited, structured set of guidelines of behavior. Stepping outside the norm would automatically then qualify and label a person atypical. Not only do these men realize they are not typical, they also recognize that they cannot speak for the majority. That is not their responsibility nor is it required or expected in this section.

The "Good Men" who contributed to this chapter have developed their explanations about what is right and wrong with relationships. Each one has his story and it is included with little editing. Their stories involve their opinions, interpretations and theories. The majority did not read the book, *If I'm Looking For A Prince, Why Am I Still Kissing Frogs*, prior to the compilation of their thoughts. It was the desire of this author to allow for free flowing, unadulterated thoughts, uninfluenced by the conclusions of my thought patterns and research. In most instances, the contributing writer agrees with and confirms the text. In others, they do not. It is neither right nor wrong. It is how they feel and perceive their experiences.

During frequent conversations, men express what a difficult burden it is trying to live up to idealistic expectations. They contend it is not that they have not tried to be what is required or that they are insensitive. It is quite the contrary. A statement made by an anonymous male acknowledges that "Our actions often qualified as borderline." Yet every action does not warrant an equal reaction. Every time a person of the male gender does something froggish, it becomes the topic of the next morning's conversation. It becomes an identification badge for all men. In the eyes of the female relating the incident, they all become frogs. Guilt by association. Men then go about business as usual, unaware of the origin of the long glares.

A new day will dawn when women, the majority, begin to understand that **Men Are Not the Enemy**. Men and women are on the same side. Men want women to talk to them, not to their mothers-in-law, or friends. Women want to talk to their men. Unless someone takes the initiative to learn and understand the process of communicating with one another, it will never happen. The facilitation of conversation must begin to create avenues for honest dialogue. With exchange, men and women will discover that what appears to be a great gulf between the genders, is actually only a small stream. A small stream that is crossable, if the desire is there. It is my observation that the desire is there and conversation has already begun. Listen In.

INTERVIEW

WITH

Albert R. Donald

On the question of relationships:

An old woman once told me there are seven (7) different kinds of people. If you have been in many relationships, you've experience one or more in each person and you learn to respond. (Did not expound on the 7 different types.) If you are in tune with who you are and go into a relationship with what you can give, you can always come out of it with something. If you give 100%, you will get 100%. The key is if a person does not give 100%, the relationship will not last.

What has been the length of your longest relationship? *Four years.*

What factors contributed to the ending of the relationships?

The goals and direction of the other person you are with are important. You must know where you want to go. We were moving in different directions. If you have dreams and aspirations and she is just interested in getting by, just surviving, it will not work. What you find is that when you are reaching a plateau, the person gets insecure. She starts saying things like, "You're going to leave me." She does not realize she is blaming the other person but it starts within herself. Women are looking for someone to make them happy - they are not looking in the mirror, to get to know the person in the mirror. When they then run into somebody that is confident, they label it as arrogance or as a better than everybody else" attitude. I see it as a person that knows where he or she is going threat. A friend once told me, "When you look for the good in a person, you will find it."

What do you look for in a person?

Most important to me are a positive attitude and an open mind. She need not be necessarily streetwise but has worldly knowledge. She is a person not afraid of taking chances in life and does not worry about the small stuff because it's all small stuff.

What advice would you give to a young woman?

Most men are looking for the prize women have. As women, you have to realize you are in control and you do not have to settle for less. Try to figure out what you want to do, where you want to go and the confidence will bring you the kind of attention you want. Men will tell you anything because they have their eyes on the prize. They'll tell you anything to win. Listen to his conversation, to what he's saying. If he's telling you, "I'll do this or I've been here and there," read between the lines. What is he not telling you, will tell you more.

Also, women, be careful with the hearts of men. It doesn't take but one time for a man to get hurt and it's the worst hurt. He perceives himself as weak because he allowed himself to become vulnerable. Men are a lot more sensitive than women believe. A man does not know how to channel that emotion. He's always taught to be tough. It hurts.

How have you handled it?

No pain, no gain. Day by day, it will go away and you learn from it. Do not react differently to a new relationship based on the pain of a previous one. Each person is different. Learn that there are things that you will accept and things you will not.

A pet peeve for me is people that cannot keep their word. A lot of women do not keep their word and they do not make decisions. When given the opportunity, they do not know what they want to do. If you do not want to go out with someone, don't do it. Say, "I am honored and glad that you took an interest in me, but I am not interested." If he acts ugly, know that he was not for you. If he is confident, he will walk away with his head up and may even continue the conversation.

What advice would you give to young men?

Bottom line: You've got your eyes on the prize but you need some kind of mental challenge. That is how we were raised. Men go through women like water and do not find what they are looking for. Go into a relationship seeing what you can give (referring to earlier statement). If you are secure with yourself, do not carry your attitude or ego on your sleeve. If she challenges your mentality, see it as a growing process. You may have more experience than the woman may but you can still learn something. Study how she thinks and feels. Do your research. Read women's magazines. What it boils down to is, what are you giving? That is what you will get back. If you are mentally stimulating, that is what you will get back. If you go in for the prize and, when you get it, you're out, it will not be a lasting relationship. Women love to be loved, to be held and treated like a queen. You want to be treated the same way, like a king. Make sure she feels like a queen. Be consistent. If you're seeing her for the first time that day, give her a kiss and a hug. If you're leaving or when you come back, give her another kiss. You never know if it is the last time that you'll be with this person. You'll know you did all you could do to love that person.

SPECIAL NOTE:

You cannot screw them all. It cannot be done. Women can be friends. It is nice having women for friends. A woman can be your access to success. You have a lot more women that are successful than men, especially in the African-American community. There are a lot of good women that can give you advice on how to be successful. Women are some of the most compassionate people on earth. If they can help, they will. Men see other men as a threat. One thing a man does not realize is professional women choose to take care of themselves by the career they select. They just want to be loved, held, to let someone take care of them. It does not matter if you work in a coal mine and she's a lawyer. If you are secure in yourself, there is not a woman out there that you cannot have.

Contributing Writer

Caryl Ford

Now hear this! Now hear this! The Princess has left the building.

When we look at where we are today, in regard to our relationships, it is so far beyond what we've learned as children. Today we see: one-parent families as the norm, divorce as the answer to marriage and the 90s woman's rejection to settling down and becoming an intimate part of a family. Society encourages her to run from it.

Underlining the separation of family is society's (the system) tools for destruction. If you marry and divorce you can actually increase your income by one third or nearly 50%, depending on how well you are able to destroy the character of the mate. The mate you once vowed to... "to thee wed".... in God's eyes.... till death do us part." The vows also state, "for better or worse," not just until things got bad. Do you understand that adversity builds inner and outer strength? (Now perhaps you know why men fear commitment: it's too expensive).

A FROG TALKS BACK

Contributing Writer

Henry Ford

Let me first thank my very special friend and Mentor for allowing me to express myself in this witty and educational book. It is not often that a frog is allowed to express itself. In fact, very often frogs are only allowed to be placed under the knife for the purpose of furthering mankind. Or perhaps more appropriately in this book, womankind.

Yes, frogs are dissected to see what makes them tick, or whatever that noise is they make. Everyone hopefully learns something he or she can remember except the frog. This book is a win-win situation. Hopefully, as you read the following pages you will learn something and I'm sure I will as well, if you will send your comments.

I should at once clear up the misconception that I am the perfect man. I know there isn't one but therein lies your salvation. If there was a perfect man and you ended up with him, what would there be to change? What fun would life be without the challenge of saving some man from himself? If you couldn't blame your mother-in-law for raising him, his sister for spoiling him, his ex-girlfriend for giving him an inflated ego and his children (from his previous marriage) for using him, what would life be like? You might actually have an equal on your hands!

All joking aside, what I share with you on the following pages is serious, even though I may at times appear to treat the subject lightly. One of my very few bits of advice on relationships is to maintain a sense of humor, and that automatically carries over into the rest of my life, including my writings.

I believe strongly in supportive and nurturing relationships. Why? Because relationships form the foundation of your life.

What you believe, what you seek, what you achieve, who you become, it is all affected by your relationships. Therefore those relationships need to be life enhancing. Most things that do not add to your life subtract from it. And it's not all take, you must also be the giver, or you become a liability and a control freak.

Whether your relationship is casual or serious, lover or friend, mate or acquaintance, the very foundation of your being is either positively affected or negatively affected by that relationship. Seldom will your relationship with someone have no affect whatsoever on you. We are all unique, changing individuals, gravitating constantly toward or away from various beliefs and philosophies.

What gives me the audacity to speak up on behalf of frogs? Ilinda Reese asks the question, "If I am looking for a Prince, why am I still kissing frogs?" I suspect that Maslow would tell us that there must be some pleasure in it. By the way, the label frog does not bother me because like most men, I have been called much worse. I do not know how you would classify me if you knew me, but certainly I would be a frog to some and a Prince to others. For the purpose of this story, I will accept the identity of the underdog.

It would help you to understand a little of my background. I was born in 1941 and raised during a time when respect was more than a song title by Areatha Franklin. There were rules for how people were to be treated, particularly young ladies. To break those rules was not a misdemeanor, or even a felony. No, to break those rules was suicide. Suicide could come in the form of a mother's backhand or neighbor's belt, but regardless, it was still suicide.

In 1951 my father passed at the young age of 40. That left my mother to raise my younger sister Jean and myself. I learned to do the things that allowed me to be self-sufficient. Yes, washing, ironing, cooking, and cleaning. No, I do not do windows. Respect and self-sufficiency have served me well over the years, but you see, these attributes never resulted in a terribly high number of girlfriends because that is not what girls were looking for! Girls

160

were looking for good dancers, sports heroes, good looks, and, would you believe, young men with good line. It should not surprise you that the young men who had what the young ladies wanted, grew up becoming proficient in dancing, sports, sometimes lying, and sometimes at least thinking, as Millie Jackson said, that they were "cuter than you." Am I jealous? I was at one time.

A cousin of mine once reflected upon the fact that the first serious loves of all five of his sisters were dancing, fast-talking, good-looking Romeo types. He noted further that each of them in time traded in their Slickum model for something much easier on the pocketbook, the ego, and life.

During a recent conversation I overheard between two female acquaintances of mine, they related how this gentleman at one of Cleveland's popular watering holes was buying $5.00 drinks. "Yeah girl, had a pocketful of money. I didn't wanna leave there." These were not inexperienced, impressionable, irrational schoolgirls. They were ladies who might more logically have been considering supporting the ego. But there they were, almost a half a century old, reinforcing the behavior that they would be deploring in the next breath. Ladies, frogs are not real smart, do not send them mixed signals.

The boys you cherished often became the men you could not stand. Even worse, based upon examples such as those in the previous paragraph, the men you cannot stand sometimes become the ones whose egos you continue to boost. Are you creating with your behavior that which you claim you do not want?

Many men cannot or will not change. Why? Quite simply because many of them are still being rewarded with your words, with your attention, your commitment and sometimes your paycheck. I know the numbers are against you, particularly in the African American community, but let me assure you that respect starts with self-respect. Demanding self-respect and setting and adhering to standards of excellence will sometimes leave you lonely, but let me remind you again that "you can do bad by yourself."

I am a witness to the last statement, because even though I thought I had the attributes to maintain a lasting relationship, I have been divorced twice. I did not let you know that in the first paragraph, because you might have shouted, "I knew he was a loser" and skipped to the next chapter. You still might skip to the next chapter, but now you've got time invested, and you know how it is when you "give" a man so many years of your life. If you have really done all the giving, perhaps you have established a pattern and helped create the monster. You have already given me a few minutes of your life so bear with me. You can have our writer-reader relationship annulled at the end of the chapter if you find our differences irreconcilable.

Today I find myself having been happily married for over ten years, and I find myself personally and professionally enhanced by the relationship. Did I do everything right in my first two marriages? Obviously not, but the foundation I rest upon today was laid during my childhood and young adult years. I am happy to issue this astounding report that I was raised not by a wife, but by a mother. I am happy also to report that I did not, and could not raise my wife. She was an independent, clear thinking individual when I met her.

I have not undergone major surgery of the mind even in my present and lasting relationship. Had my wife been looking for a dancing, debonair, wad-of-money carrying, super popular mate to spend her life with, she would not have stopped at me. It is surprising and disturbing how many of our female friends and acquaintances assume that any of my positive attributes are a result of my wife training me.

When the ladies reading this book become the mother-in-laws of their son's wives, please do not forget to remember. Remember that what your son does wrong will likely be blamed upon you having spoiled him. Remember that what he does right

162

will be credited to your daughter-in-law. Heaven forbid if he was to be responsible for anything himself.

So the question I leave you with after this brief encounter is "Are you looking for a frog to be happy with, or a Prince to be happy with?" Or are you, like many that have failed before, looking for a frog to change into a Prince, or a Prince to change into a frog?

If you are looking for either one to change into the other, I caution you that you are going against the irrevocable laws of nature and the basic concept of reason. Those laws include but are not limited to the fact that an abject in motion tends to stay at rest. Those laws include the fact that rewarded behavior tends to create patterns, which become habits, which become a personality.

Those concepts include the fact that most of us are surrounded by people somewhat like ourselves in circumstances that characterize who we are. We are surrounded and blanketed by a support system that reinforces who we are, so changing us is not like the fourteen-day recipe of how to break a habit. Frogs and Princes have different aspirations.

There are different strokes for different folks, so I urge you to make certain that you really want what you do not have, before you trade in what you do have. As my dear and smarter-than-me sister puts it "Be careful what you pray for, because you just might get it."

About the writer -- Henry Ford is a motivational speaker and the author of *Success Is You and The Power of Association.*

Contributing Writer

C. Hall Jr.

For those of you looking for that "Prince";

To attract the best, you have to think of the best and always truly believe that the best does exist. Not just exist, but exist for you.

I get tired of hearing the same old, sad song, "there are no good men available." If this is your thinking, you are destined to attract nothing because that is what your mind is focused on. It occurs especially when there is a group of you and you comfort one another with negativity. Maybe it's **you**. There are a lot of good men out here but they are not always obvious. They may need encouragement and support. For example, Denzale Washington probably would not be where he is today if it were not for that special woman who brought out the best in him. It takes a team to make royalty. If a royal family is the result you seek, open your eyes, your heart, and your mind. Because whether you believe it or not,

What you are actively thinking,
You are physically seeking.

Young, strong, male, persistently positive!

Contributing Writer

Clifferd Eugene Lee

Clifferd Eugene Lee is an artist, the creator of the book cover and a valuable source of wisdom. Despite this introduction, he does not perceive himself to be a writer, though eloquent in speech. Therefore, the following excerpts were obtained from information provided over the past year. Clifferd's comments often reflect, confirm and are representative of the male's point of view and feelings.

Listen in on his conversation:

Lack of men?

Yes, I believe there is a lack of men. When I say men, I am speaking from a spiritual viewpoint. I am speaking of men who know, study, live, teach and preach the word, etc....Righteous men are my topic. The rest do not matter.

I am aware of the male ego and also aware of our foolish acts that are derived from our egos (pride). I want to be true to myself so that I can be true to others.

Women...
I believe you, as women, just want to be loved and set free to find yourselves. Set free to discover the elements about you. Yes, you want family and all that it offers yet you also need time for self-interest. Then, if it happens, that you find you now have time for self-interest, there is no one of interest to share it fully with.

I have always been one to handle my problems alone and to help others. Over the past six years, I have learned that sometimes

I need help also. All in all, I am a good provider to my loves and often spoil them to no end.

A wife is the better half of the man. Men need to take time to realize that a woman is a help meet and not a piece of meat.

The Physical? (Admits to previously being a womanizer).

Sex is great but I have found it to be empty without a true foundation. Yes, it has its momentary pleasures but it has also given me long- term headaches, if you know what I mean. I enjoy the mental stimulation of an intelligent woman.

The Princess and the frog scenario...

All too often I have seen and have been a part of such situations. In each one, the lies never prevailed. I found the factors influencing an element of trust were based upon words and not deeds. This Princess trusted the frog because of his verbal showing of intellect. No matter how intelligent, this frog's words lacked something (truth). So in actuality, the story became illustrative of the biblical narrative of Jesus in the desert with Satan. In both situations, false words prevailed -- Not. Clever words were used to attempt to obtain some interest or prize but nothing prevails like the truth. I found several small messages in the "Princess and the frog" dialogue alone.

Clifferd E. Lee insists, as the others, that he is not a frog, but a Prince. He based his statement on his spiritual foundation and supported it with scripture.

True Love...Is of God

The scripture says that God is spirit and that God is love. If we are made in the image of God then we are spirit and our spirit is love. So, in our travels through life, our souls come across various

166

types of love that need to be expressed. One type of such expression of love is the song in ballot form. The song of love is the truest expression of the soul's cries unto the spirit for love. Once the soul's message of love is delivered to the spirit, it is transformed into a song of love. It is the inner conveyance of that which God has commanded human life to express -- Love.

After viewing the movie, _Waiting to Exhale_, Clifferd composed and offers the following soliloquy for consideration:

I'VE TRIED

Over the years I've tried to find love. I've searched in many common and unusual places. I've even sacrificed to that which I thought was righteous and true.

Love, it was not in the lures of the opposite sex,

I've tried.

Love, was not given in the lust of the heart,

I've tried.

Love, was not found in fornication,

I've tried.

Love, was not found in the arms of any woman,

I've tried.

And as time passed and wrong choices taken, I've lost the will to search for foolish love. Yet, now I know what True Love is all about. It is kindness, patience, hope, truth, trust, perseverance, and protection. These are the attributes of love. For love is God and God is a spirit and we are made in his likeness (spirit). Therefore, true love dwells within our spirit, which ultimately is God's love.

It's taken many years for me to find love and I know that you too are searching.

One day, maybe you will know the truth, Why?

Because, I've tried!

LADIES: SET YOUR STANDARDS

Contributing Writer

Randell McShepard

Time after time I have heard women use the expression, "A good man is hard to find." What does this mean? Well, **_Webster's Dictionary_** defines the word "find" as "to discover accidentally." Hmmm. Maybe we should change the expression to "A good man is hard to discover accidentally." Now that's more befitting!

Many women far too often are not sure or clear about what they really want in a relationship or in a man. As a result, they haphazardly enter relationships that are destined to fail. And after a few negative experiences with relationships, they find resolve in saying to girlfriends, "A good man is hard to find" or "Where are the good men?"

Women seeking to find what they would determine to be a good man should first do an assessment. An assessment of self. What do you want?   What is more important to you in a relationship?   Many women say that they want men that are established and very successful, but are they themselves scuffling to make ends meet. If you are scuffling, why not consider a "good" man in the same position?   Some say they want a man who is spiritual, but need themselves to grow spiritually.   Why not consider a man that could grow spiritually with you? Others say they want a non-abusive, loving man, but have spent years with just the opposite, and as a result are bitter, humiliated and frustrated.

Ladies, decide what your standards are and *hold firm to them*. If a man does not meet your standards, *do not waste your time or his*. If you know you are only dating him for looks, don't act surprised when the intellect you may desire is not there. If you are attracted only to his money, do not act disappointed when you discover that the trust and communication that you are used to is not there.

Family values, spirituality, trust, communication, congeniality, humor, responsibility, and work ethics. These are the qualities and/or criteria by which women should select their partners. That is, if they truly want healthy and long-lasting relationships.

A final question:

Do you prefer to meet, evaluate, establish a friendship, and fall in love with the man of your dreams or to take your chances on "accidentally discovering" your man?

THE CHOICE IS YOURS.

The Thoughts of

Contributing Writer

James Oliver

On Relationships...

A relationship is only as good as its communication. Communication can be expressed verbally (through words) or expressed non-verbally. People communicate their thoughts through their mouths and their feelings through their bodies.

Communication is a meeting of meanings. If your desire is to communicate, never answer a question with a question, unless you are seeking clarification. Make sure everyone you are attempting to communicate with, is speaking the same language. The difference between men and women goes beyond the physical characteristics. Men and women bond differently with each other. A man can bring things out of a woman that another woman cannot. A woman can bring out of a man what another man cannot. However, you cannot make someone do something they do not want to do. People, generally speaking, do not change.

Do not dish out any medicine you cannot take yourself. Do not expect anything from someone that you are not willing to give yourself. Treat others like you want to be treated.

The two main ingredients of a relationship are love and honesty. Sometimes it is better to be loving than to be right

Make a covenant between one another. A covenant is defined three ways:

Definition:

An agreement entered into by two or more persons or parties.

Biblically:

It is God's promise of blessing to be fulfilled, on the performance of a condition.

Law:

Legally, it is an agreement between parties under seal.

If you are presently in a relationship, turn and face your mate. Make a covenant between you, by repeating the following affirmation to each other:

I regard you and myself as being created in the image of God.

I see your beauty.

I sense your power.

I celebrate your potential.

I support your prerogative to sing your song.

I share your pursuit of a high quality of life.

I will tell you the truth and I will have your trust.

I will listen to you with my heart.

And I shall speak to you with my smile.

I shall care enough to confront and comfort you.

In you I see God and in God I see you.

You are my friend and I love you.

Now hug each other to seal the covenant. Next, consider the following anonymous advice for application to relationships and life:

LIVE A LITTLE RECKLESSLY

If you stop giving the moment it begins to hurt,

> You will never discover true generosity.

If you stop serving the moment it pinches you,

> You will never discover sacrifice and its rewards.

If you quit loving the moment it becomes difficult, you will never experience the meaning of passion.

If you refuse to forgive in the moment that it cries for revenge, you will never discover the grace of unconditional forgiveness.

If you hesitate to share yourself the moment it cost, you will never discover intimate fellowship.

Joy comes to the one who does not know when to quit: Who can't draw a line, who can give, love and live

A little recklessly.

Remember the following bits of practical suggestions:

- The right type of togetherness is based upon the right type of separateness. An example of this statement is the egg theory. When holding an egg, one must not hold too tight or it will crush the egg. If held too loose, one loses control and may also destroy the egg. In relationships, it is important to have the right grip. The objective is to help the other person to be everything they can be.

- People play like they practice. People generally do not change.

- Do not start what you cannot finish.

- After marriage, the courtship should continue. Marriage should be an outgrowth of the courting.

- The best is the enemy of the good.

- Always put your best foot forward.

- Do not travel the waters without the proper equipment. To fish, one needs the proper vessel. The vessel is determined by the objectives that you want to achieve. To achieve optima's performance, you must have both oars in the water at the same time. Fishing requires the right time of day and season. In relationships, you cannot attract the right fish with the wrong bait. To be successful, you must exercise patience.

Contributing writer

Minister Ronald Pettigrew

The foundation of a true relationship rests upon love. All other foundations are sinking sand. If a relationship is to be of any lasting value then the motive can neither be self-centered, nor based upon mere practical reasoning.

The direct cause of a marriage should not be for security, money, publicity, prestige, or lust, if you please. These temporal things will not weather the storms of life. We do ourselves an injustice and Holy Matrimony of its God truth, when we confess the "I Do" under such false pretense.

When a man findeth a woman, it is simply marvelous. He findeth a good thing; a pearl. Behold a found treasure in an earthen vessel. When a woman chooseth to love a man, of her own free will, then it is simply wonderful. For she has found whom her soul loveth and will not let him go. He has become her "Hero." A good relationship must be built upon truth, loyalty, and respect. It is recognizing respect in each other as it is exposed.

Communication is the number one factor for a successful relationship. Communication involves listening and hearing what the other has to say. A mutual respect.

These are a few requirements for building a good relationship. It is getting to know one another, day by day, for as long as you live. No one should know you as well as your mate. It is discovering your favorite color, dessert, flower, etc.

When a man loves a woman, he is to love her even as Christ loves the Church and even as the man loveth himself. Not his own definition of love, but a true commitment to her, to love to cherish, to protect, to serve, until death do us part.

IN DEFENSE OF PRINCESSES

AND

FROGS

Contributing Writer

Kofi Makana Omawale Seru

Many of us, at least those of my age group, were raised on fairy tales. Our introduction to reading often included a copy of *Grimms Fairy Tales* or such books. Aside from the obvious cultural biases and racial coloration, inherent in these texts, fairy tales often served as our first lesson and interpretation of societies' ideas of morals and values.

The story of the Princess and Frog, I believe, relates the reality of the transformational power of love. Of course, the crux of that interpretation lies in one's definition of love. I see love as a concept encompassing many elements, the sum of which is greater than the individual parts. Love is not a kiss, a touch, a look, a feeling, passion/lust, respect, patience, selflessness, empathy, physical, or spiritual attraction. It cannot be reduced to any one of these.

Love is the combined presence and force of all of these plus the mystery. As such, it has transforming powers. Love can only be experienced but never fully defined. Like God, it is always more than we believe it to be.

Contrary to popular opinions, transformations, when dealing with human beings, does not occur immediately. In this hurry up, fast- food, self-serve, quick-fix oriented society, we have come to expect instant change, instant gratification and instant success. The human psyche is much too complex to allow for that.

176

Immediate change results in negative effects and mental breakdowns. In relationship they often spell doom.

It is important to note here, that in the context of the myth, the frog and the Princess are being transformed by love. The Princess is asked to set aside, if only temporarily, her perception of herself, her individual and perhaps cultural aversion to the frog and her vanity. The frog is required to have faith and to make himself vulnerable to another.

My friend, the author of this brave and uniquely provocative liberating text, has made available to the reader the building blocks of a healthy relationship. If they are used diligently and in the spirit of commitment, success in relations can be increased.

In my twenty-five years of marriage, I have used and sometimes abused some of these building blocks. I have selected many according to my particular needs and the dictates of circumstances. The one block which I pick up first and most frequently is the block of commitment. I feel safe in adding through twenty-five years of marriage, that it is my wife's most treasured block too. We may at times knock over the pile but commitment is the block we cling to and upon which we rebuild.

In conclusion, if ever there was a frog (ribbit) it was I. The product of: a broken home, alcoholic parents, frequent verbal abuse, low, and sometimes, no self-esteem. Many of my good qualities were hidden and inert. I give thanks every day that my fairy Princess removed her crown, looked into my heart and soul and decided that I was worth the effort. She saw the Prince in me, miraculously, sees it still. Every day she transforms me with her love.

Contributing Writer

Massimo Stark

I believe that the key to relationship is learning to pay attention. By paying attention, I don't mean obligatory listening to someone about the facts of her day. I mean softening your own eyes and ears so you can take the other person in freshly, almost like you'd never taken them in before. If people can do that for and with each other on a regular basis, everything is possible. Problems get solved. Adjustments occur. And the relationship is continuously reinvented.

Lillian Hellman said once, "I know as little about romantic love as I did at 18, but I do know about the deep pleasure of continuing interest, the excitement of wanting to know what somebody else thinks, will do, will not do; the tricks played and unplayed, the short cord that the years make into a rope."

Real paying attention generally requires people to take turns. When one person is experiencing a lot of emotion, they will not be able to pay great attention to the other until they are attended to. If the couple understands this and maintains equity; the relationship will grow and prosper. If one person is continuously demanding unilateral attention, the relationship will mutate or wither.

Mutually paying attention leads to knowing and being known. Really known. Intimacy is about deep knowing and being known. For some reason I do not entirely understand, women and men act differently about this. Most women are deeply attracted to knowing and being known. If their man is game for this, most women, in my experience, have an almost infinite capacity for loving what they find... even when it is problematic or painful.

Most men, on the other hand, act on a week-to-week, month-to-month basis as if deeply knowing and being known is something to be avoided at all costs. I am frankly not sure where this fear comes from. I do know that deep down most men find knowing and being known just as pleasurable as women. When something calamitous happens and the man is forced into sharing himself and taking in his woman, he experiences a deep pleasure and asks himself why he waited so long. But the same man often goes right back to avoiding this kind of intimate contact on a day-to-day basis like the plague. Many women grow tired of this imbalance and give up.

My advice is not revolutionary. Patience. A willingness to wait for opportunities. Talking about the pleasure of real contact when it occurs so learning seeps in.

Good luck and here is an excerpt from a poem I like, that relates to this, by *William Stafford*:

"If you don't know the kind of person I am and I don't know the kind of person you are a pattern that others made may prevail in the world and following the wrong god home we miss our star. For there is many a small betrayal in the mind, a shrug that lets the fragile sequence break sending with shouts the horrible errors of childhood storming out to play through the broken dike."

Contributing Writer

Robert Swain

I am not a frog! Let's make this clear from the beginning. Though I must confess that at times in my life I may have croaked and ate flies and even hopped around a little, I am not a frog.

Strong willed, driven and destined for glory, you have not only grown into the roles of leadership and power but also made homes for our children. I salute you. Without your efforts over the last few centuries the Black population of the country would be nothing. As your standards raise, individually and as a group, you look for a mate that will at least be your equal. This can be no easy task considering the challenges facing black men in America today.

Many of you end up having to settle for a brother that you hope has the capabilities to live up to the "potential" that you see in him. This is your frog. Not really the man, but your idea of what he could be. You say, "All I have to do is kiss him." Yeah, that may work for a moment but he still is who he is. You then find out that you have to keep kissing and kissing and kissing him, trying to keep your dreams and his "potential" from fading into reality. It is not hard to see how tired and frustrated you both can become. Eventually you find a new frog to kiss. It is a never-ending story.

How do we (and I say "we" because we Princes are waiting for you) solve this problem? I believe there are three basic things that have to be done:

•   First and foremost we have to become "fully" spiritually aware. Fully means we have to learn to live the ways of our maker. It means to be at peace with ourselves, learning how to love and be loved. Too often we look at the worldly aspects (sex, money, material things.) of a relationship as the basis for its growth. Although these are important, they are not the foundation on which

180

a strong partnership can be built. When we strengthen our spirituality, our vision becomes clearer and we see past the "could" do (frog) to the "is "doing (Prince).

•Second, all that glitters isn't gold. We have heard this many times but it seems that we still go for the outer beauty and not the substance of the individual. Physical appearance plays an important part in the initial attraction, but there is no staying power in looks alone. Too often we reach for the shiny apple on the tree passing up sweeter and juicier fruit along the way. Then, when we do not get what we expected, we say the whole tree is bad and go on to look elsewhere. So what we need to do is take our time to look at what is before us. Look at the lifestyle and commitment of potential mates and how they compare to our own. Time will be our greatest ally in finding the Princes' among the frog.

What is left for us to do is something that we do not need to build on but breakdown and these are expectations. This is critical we have all had dreams and fantasies about our ideal mate. These are good because they keep our standards high and that is the way it should be. Again, though we do not want to limit ourselves to what may never happen, remember, "The perfect person for you will not be perfect." They will have flaws that you may or may not like. Things in time, you may get used to or may want to change. Who could ever think that the person you have been waiting your whole life for, could have such gross-looking toenails and snore. Who could ever think that his idea of a great Sunday afternoon is not going shopping.

This is such a short and simple answer to a complicated question. If I knew all the answers I would have a better relationship now. The truth is that we must truly love ourselves before we can even begin to find true love from someone else.

These are just some of the things we need to work on as Princes and Princess if we want to get our castles in order and live happily ever after. It can be done!

Peace and love,

The Prince formally known as,

Robert Swain

P. S. "I'm still marchin."

Contributing Writer

M. D. Walker

Human relationships are fragile. Breakable in an instant. Human relationships are resilient; bouncing past the heartbreaks.

Yet when a man has found the companionship of a woman, a treasure to be held up through time, the relationship then becomes arduous. A thing to "work at."

Sadly, "work at" is becoming increasingly less fashionable in our modern times. Still, the modern times we find ourselves in, will become the past and replaced by yet another modern time. Who is to say that the future will find people more willing to "work at" it?

After all, what does one do when, in his mind, he believes he has done all the work he can, on the present relationship? Just what is "all the work?" How long does it take to achieve?

I have given 14 years of my life to this relationship-building process between a man and a woman. After experiencing some bumps, bouncing past heartbreaks, decided it was fragile and broke it off in an instant. But was it fragile? Was it worth the time invested, just to break it off in an instant? One thing is for sure; the jury is still out.

Each and every one of us will have to determine what our relationships will be like. How much time will we spend developing each?? What will eventually cause us to sever one and move to another? Ah yes, moving on to yet another relationship. Arduous? Yes! But it seems to be very fashionable in our modern times.

Human relationships: Fragile, resilient, breakable, bouncing. Truly a lesson in ourselves; Who are we and what we stand for. Stand for something -- Lest we fall for anything! Human relationship was once the subject of a poem I composed. It describes the way I want all of my relationships to be. I hope you read it. Here it is:

YOU & ME

You; A person able to overcome all major and minor confrontations

Me; A person willing to adjust to any and every situation

They; They are looking on with only one anticipation

That we, you and me, find happiness amid security

Through the love we show

Let us grow

To the depth of love so sure

It is bound to be secure.

Whatever this turns out to be
It's on You & Me. M. D. Walker, A gentleman, a simple man

A nugget candy commercial opens with a frog hopping and changing. The commercial promises "you that are in search for Mr. Right, you'll run into small-minded (the frog changes into a dinosaur) but not a single Prince Charming."
The men in this section contend that they are not frogs. They are human beings, just trying to get it right. They are not void of irritating habits, yet their flaws do not diminish their character. They are men who fight through their fears in an attempt to regain their roles and responsibilities. Though it is understood that they (the men in this chapter) do not desire to speak for the masses, their voices will speak for the millions that are not presented yet represented. Good men who respond to women:

In a firm yet fair way

Protective yet liberating

Loving but not always agreeing.

They are Good men who are willing to become part of the solution by initiating dialogue that will lead to better understanding and communication. It is the hope of the contributing writers that their insights will prove to be thought provoking and enlightening.

After reading the various excerpts you may again pose the question, "Where are these Good men?" "How can I meet them?" The dramatic conclusion of this chapter could be to provide the addresses and phone numbers of the eligible men. This book could then join the ranks of _Ebony_ magazine or Match Makers Inc. in supplying and creating matches made in heaven. The objective of the chapter is not to focus on the name or personality of the person but the content presented. It is to create an awareness that yes, Good men do exist. It may seem hard to find that special one for whom you long. However, if you open your eyes, you may find one standing right in front of you.

CHAPTER 8

AND THEY LIVED

HAPPILY-EVER-AFTER ?

"We had a fairy tale romance"
And a diamond like this promises
We'll live happily-ever-after.

Promises, like these words, from an advertisement for a gem company, promise the stereotypical expectation that is possible, even probable, for a couple to live "Happily-ever-after."

As with every fairy tale you read as a child, every couple in the story came to the expected conclusion. A new compilation of fairy tales revealed a new twist to the standard ending. The change in wording from the original version first published in 1812 reflects the changing times. The wording reads:

"And they lived happily a great many years."

Throughout this book, the attempt has been to destroy fantasy and deal with reality. The "real" story does not begin with once upon-a-time. It does not end with your riding off into the sunset on a white horse with your Prince Charming. It does not end with your handsome husband positioning you in a white house with a picket fence, two-car garage (Corvette in the yard) with 2.5 children. Though the above may describe your future, the reality is marriage is hard work.

REALITY CHECK:

How many couples do you know that lived happily ever after? How can there be a happily-ever-after in the middle?

Marriage is a continual growth process, complete with new challenges and struggles.

This Section is Optional

Be Careful: Reading It May Change Your Life

FOREVER!

INQUIRING

MINDS WANT

TO KNOW...

Inquiring minds often ask questions of the author that are of a personal nature. The search to know more leads them to ask, "Are you married? Are you in love? Is there a man in your life? The object of their questions is to help them determine the credibility of the information and the source of the insights presented.

Yes, I am in love and He's in love with me. He has the wisdom of the ages and always looks out for my best interests. He tells me I am beautiful and wonderfully made and he loves me just the way I am. In fact, He loved me before I could love myself. He gave me his love before I was willing to accept it. He takes care of me better than I can take care of myself. He is wealthy beyond this world and He supplies my needs according to his riches. He tells me that nothing I could ever say or do would cause him to ever leave me. I have never known anyone as faithful as He is. He's never late and He has never disappointed me. Yes, He is my Lover.

Are you still curious to know who can make such promises and keep them? Want to know his name? His name is ......Jesus Christ.

Are you now saying, "Okay Ilinda, that's all good but what is the real scope? Are you saying you're married to Jesus and have no need for a man?" No, in the natural there is presently (depending on when you purchase this book) one man that touches my heart in a special way. He contains the characteristics I require in an individual I want to spend time with. Want to know who **he** **is**?? He does too. He is also waiting (along with several hopefuls) for the answer. Sorry. These pages will not reveal the answer. Why not? Think about it. If I told you who and where these men are that possess all five of the characteristics I seek, you'd beat me to their doors.

More importantly than the information provided above, is this:

My love interest is not as important as being able to now love myself. The knowledge of loving myself allows me to be confident in my destiny. If the apple of my eye, the present focus of my attention, calls tomorrow and says the familiar phrase, "I'm getting married" or "Can we just be friends," I can answer without reservation: Yes. The fulfillment of my life is not dependent on an external source. Yes, there would be a time of healing, evaluating and internalizing what occurred but it would soon lead to celebrating what the future holds for me.

Another writer said it best,

> "And there comes the time that as we live, we learn, we laugh, we sigh and then we try again."

READING LIST

Astrachan, Anthony, How Men Feel: Their Response to Women's Demands for Equality and Power, Anchor Press/Doubleday, 1986.

Baraff, Alvin, Dr., Men Talk, How Men Really Feel About Women, Sex, Relationships and Themselves.

Bloomfield, Harold MD and Vettese, Sirah Ph. D., Lifemates: The Love Fitness Program for a Lasting Relationship, 1989.

Bray, Semia, Love, Loving and Being Loved, Published by Noisemaker, 1996.

Browne, Joy Dr., Why They Don't Call When They Say They Will -- And Other Mixed Signals, Simon and Schuster, New York, N.Y.

Brown, Les, Live Your Dreams.

Cabot, Tracey, Ph. D., Marrying Later, Marrying Smarter, McGraw-Hill Publishing Co., 1990.

Cutter, Rebecca, When Opposites Attract. Right Brain/Left Brain Relationships and How to Make Them Work, Dutton Book, Published by the Penguin Group, 1994.

Cypert, Samuel A., The Power of Self-Esteem, A WorkSmart Book (Workbook) Series.
The American Management Association, 1994.

Same author, How to Keep A Man In Love With You Forever, McGraw-Hill Book Co, 1986.

DeAngelis, Barbara Ph. D., Are You the One For Me?, Delacorte Press, 1992.

Dobson, James Dr., Love Hunger.

Dowling, Collette, The Cinderella Complex, Women's Hidden Fear of Independence, Published by Summit Books.

Forward, Susan and Torres, Joan, Men Who Hate Women and the Women that Love Them.

Same author, Toxic Parents.

Fromme, Allan, The Ability To Love. The Sleeping Giant Within.

Gray, John, Ph.D., What Your Mother Couldn't Tell You and Your Father Didn't Know, 1994.

Gaylin, Willard, M.D., The Male Ego, Published by Penguin Group, copyright 1992.

Hanlon O,' Bill and Hudson, Pat, Love Is a Verb, WW Norton & Co. NY/London.

Harper, Phillip Brian, Are We Not Men? Masculine Anxiety and the Problem of African American Identity. A Sociological Study.

Hendricks, Harville, Ph. D., Getting the Love You Want and Keeping the Love You Find.

Hite, Shere and Knopf, Alfred A., The Hite Report on Male Sexuality.

Jacklin, Carol Nagy, Ph. D., The Psychology of Sex Differences. Long, Courtney, Love Awaits, African Women Talk About Sex, Love and Life, A Bantam Book, 1995.

Margulis, Lynn and Sagan, Dorion, Mystery Dance on the Evolution of Human Sexuality,
Summit Books.

194

Marion, Ross, Removing Your Mask.

Overlook, Joy, Love Stinks., The Romantic's Guide To Breaking Up Without Breaking Down, Pocket Books, a Division of Simon & Schuster Inc., 1990.

Paley, Vivian G., Boys and Girls: Superheros in the Doll Corner.

Patterson, Ella, Will The Real Women....Please Stand Up!! Uncommon Sense About Self-Esteem, Self-Discovery, Sex and Sensuality. A Self Help Book.

Price, Stephen, Dr. and Price, Susan, No More Lonely Nights.

Reynolds, A.L. III, Do Black Women Hate Black Men?, 1994.

Russianoff, Penelope, Dr., Why Do I Think I'm Nothing Without A Man: A New Guide to Rationale Living.

Taylor, Susan, In the Spirit.

Weiner-Davis, Michelle, Divorce Busting: A Step-By-Step Approach to Making Your Marriage Loving Again.

Williamson, Marianne, A Return To Love.

same author, A Woman's Worth.

Young-Eisendrath, Polly, Ph. D., You're Not What I Expected.